MW01001006

"I LOVE this book. It ha
friendship across faiths,
stories of vision turned into
brought me back to the core idea behind Interfaith roo...
traditions call on us to serve others, and there is no greater joy or
more important task than to do so together. Thank you to everyone
involved in this project for this gift to the world."

— Eboo Patel, Founder and President, Interfaith Youth Core

"This poignant look into the heart of our various religious traditions
is a celebration of the power of The Holy moving in us and through
us in many voices and spiritual traditions. Telling stories, human
stories, helps lead us into faith-filled celebration of our differences
as grace marks and reminds us to do the work of everyday justice."

— Emilie M. Townes, Dean and E. Rhodes and Leona B.
Carpenter Professor of Womanist Ethics and Society,
Vanderbilt University Divinity School

"Read this book and feel God tapping you on the shoulder every few
pages, as I did. Youthful voices finding wisdom in their friendships,
pain, and questions, alongside experienced faith leaders surprised
by the joy of discovering justice in new corners as they wrestle
their faith to the ground."

— Rob Wilson-Black, CEO, Sojourners

"*Acting on Faith: Stories of Courage, Activism, and Hope across
Religions* shares powerful and inspiring stories of real people,
doing important community work, from diverse backgrounds and
experiences. Faires Beadle and Haskins illustrate the commonality
of our values and struggles in the midst of our diversity. A must
read for those doing interfaith work."

— Kim Bobo, Executive Director, Virginia Interfaith Center for
Public Policy

"Most people, no matter how many newspapers they read or diverse Twitter feeds they follow, hear only a tiny percentage of the stories this world and its people have to tell. We mostly hear stories from others like us, whose lives and neighborhoods and daily struggles look a good deal like our own. Such is the particularity of human life, which seems only exacerbated by recent political and cultural polarization. *Acting on Faith: Stories of Courage, Activism, and Hope across Religions* grants readers access to life changing stories offered in truly diverse voices. Though the responses to the most pressing challenges and questions of our age are unsurprisingly varied across religious traditions, the good will, self-reflection, and commitment to interfaith justice work articulated by each contributor promises a future—and present—in which that polarization can be transformed. Faires Beadle and Haskins have assembled a hope-filled and very necessary resource."

— Bromleigh McCleneghan, Associate Pastor, Union Church of Hinsdale, author of *Good Christian Sex: Why Chastity Isn't the Only Option and Other Things the Bible Says About Sex,* coauthor of *Hopes and Fears: Everyday Theology for New Parents and Other Tired, Anxious People,* coeditor of *When Kids Ask Hard Questions: Faith-Filled Responses for Tough Topics*

ACTING ON FAITH

STORIES OF COURAGE, ACTIVISM, AND HOPE ACROSS RELIGIONS

DIANE FAIRES BEADLE &
JAMIE LYNN HASKINS, editors

chalice
press

Saint Louis, Missouri

An imprint of Christian Board of Publication

Quotations from the Bible, unless otherwise marked, are from the *New Revised Standard Version Bible,* copyright 1989, Division of Christian Education of the National Council of the Churches of Christ in the United States of America. Used by permission. All rights reserved.

Quotations from the Qur'an indicate the English translation they are from. The translations can be found at https://www.islamawakened.com/index.php.

Hadith quotations are from https://www.islamicfinder.org/hadith.

Quotations from the Torah marked Sefaria are from https://www.sefaria.org.

Cover design: Jennifer Pavlovitz

ChalicePress.com

Print 9780827200890

EPUB 9780827200906

EPDF 9780827200913

Printed in the United States of America

Contents

Introduction

Diane's inspiration for this project:

It was a rainy, dreary day on the Habitat for Humanity construction site, but warm laughter and a sense of joy was palpable in spite of the weather. A few of the volunteers, like the friendly women from the Hindu temple, barely knew how to hold a hammer. Others, like the two Buddhist monks in orange robes, could have built the whole house by themselves. A Sikh man used duct tape to keep his hard hat securely fastened over his turban, and the young Imam decided to take off his long, black robe so he could more easily assemble the studs that were turning into walls around us. This, I thought as I looked around, is what I imagine the kingdom of God looks like. People of all kinds, united—and delighted—by our efforts to create safe, affordable housing for a neighbor in need. We were all motivated to be there on that cold, wet morning by the principles of our faith, which had taught us through different stories and sacred scriptures why we should care about the well-being of a stranger.

As a child, I grew up acting out the story of the good Samaritan (Luke 10:25–37) at church camp. Christian Bible verses like "love your neighbor as yourself" and "I was hungry and you gave me food" are deeply ingrained in my memory. I felt a call to ministry, in large part, because of the example of clergy and churches in low-income communities that were making a tangible difference in people's lives.

Although religion gets a lot of negative attention these days for inspiring hatred, violence, and division, in my experience religion

1

moves many more ordinary people to acts of love, generosity, and selflessness every day. The world is filled with young Muslim men like Deah Barakat, a dental student at the University of North Carolina, who was inspired to organize a free dental clinic for Syrian refugees. Tragically, Deah, his wife, and his sister-in-law were killed by a neighbor because of the very religion that taught them to serve others.[1]

When I heard the news about the murder of these three compassionate young people, I felt compelled to do something. I knew Deah's brother, Farris, because we had both helped organize the first Interfaith Habitat for Humanity build in Raleigh, North Carolina. I have been inspired to continue volunteering and speaking out for justice by colleagues and neighbors who are Muslim, Jewish, Hindu, Sikh, and Buddhist. I have even discovered that my own faith is deepened and renewed by their example and commitment to their faith, as I have worked alongside them. It is my deepest hope that others may also find inspiration for putting their faith into action through the witness of people like Deah, Farris, and the countless other faithful people working to address the problems our communities face.

Diane Faires Beadle *loves bringing people of various cultures and faiths together. She volunteers with Habitat for Humanity of Wake County's annual Interfaith Build. Diane was raised in the Christian Church (Disciples of Christ) and serves as Senior Minister at St. Paul's Christian Church in Raleigh, North Carolina. A graduate of Vanderbilt Divinity School and Rhodes College, Diane was born in Texas, grew up in Germany, and considers Tennessee home. She also has a great love for Sri Lanka, where she spent two years teaching English. She and her husband Michael enjoy hiking, running, cooking spicy foods, and traveling the world.*

Jamie Lynn's inspiration for this project:

She walked into my office and sat down on the couch with a sigh. "I don't want to talk to you because you're a Christian," she said under her breath, "but now I really need someone to talk to and you're the only one who's here." I'm a college chaplain and many

---

[1]Ashley Fantz, "Slain North Carolina couple and sister remembered as generous, loving." *CNN*. http://www.cnn.com/2015/02/11/us/chapel-hill-shooting-victims/index.html

students find their way to my office to laugh or cry and share what's going on in their lives. This young woman, however, had been avoiding me at all costs. She was Muslim and a part of the LGBTQIA+ (lesbian, gay, bisexual, transgender, queer, intersex, asexual) community and, in her words, "Christians hate gay people and they hate Muslims."

She was right, I am a Christian. But she was also wrong. I do not hate gay people or Muslims. In fact, I am a part of the LGBTQIA+ community and I have a deep respect for Islam and the people who practice it. As she settled herself on my office couch, I desperately wanted her to know that my faith tradition teaches me that all people are beloved. They are good and they are worthy of great love and respect. I follow Jesus, in part, because of the radical welcome and hospitality he offers everyone. But how could she know this without hearing my story? Tales of religious hatred and division often fill our newsfeed. At Pride parades across the country and the world, it is Christians holding signs of exclusion and hate, and it is Christians, in part, who spread harmful messages about Islam. In this moment I realized the importance of sharing our stories, the truths about who we are, in all of our beautiful complexity.

My students are Buddhist, Hindu, Jewish, Muslim, Atheist, Agnostic, Christian, and everything in between. Until we sit down together in offices, coffee shops, classrooms, or neighborhood parks and share ourselves and our stories, we cannot truly know one another. Our experiences provide a look into our theological commitments and understanding of the holy. In our current world, with so many false narratives and assumptions, the sharing of stories is work I feel deeply called to do.

Jamie Lynn Haskins *delights in people and their stories, particularly those shared across faith traditions. She serves on the board of the Virginia Interfaith Center for Public Policy. Jamie Lynn is ordained in the Christian Church (Disciples of Christ) and serves as Chaplain for Spiritual Life at the University of Richmond. Before moving to Richmond, Jamie Lynn served as Chaplain, Director of the Center for Faith & Service, and Instructor at Westminster College in Fulton, Missouri, and is proud to share the stories of several Westminster students here in this book. She is a member of Seventh Street Christian Church (Disciples of Christ) and enjoys camping, cooking, and exploring her new hometown of Richmond, Virginia, with her trusty pup Bernie.*

Our hope:

This book is a celebration of the many faiths that call us to reach out, speak up, lend a hand, and appreciate the beauty of humanity. It's not the story of "us" versus "them." Rather, it looks at the heart of the world's religious traditions; it examines the core of who we are as people of faith through our stories; and it seeks to build bridges across many divides. This book celebrates our differences and explores the countless ways we are connected, as all of us strive to stand up for justice, to side with the oppressed, and to tell the stories of our faith. As you get a glimpse into the experiences of your diverse neighbors working for justice, we hope you will gain deeper insights into how your own faith motivates you to respond to the challenging questions of modern life.

Our conversation unfolds in six chapters. Each focuses on a social justice issue our faith calls us to address: immigration, sexism, racism, sexual orientation and gender identity, religious extremism, and care for the environment. We explore each issue through personal stories from across faith traditions, and together, as Christians and Jews, Muslims and Buddhists, Hindus and Pagans, we examine how our deepest beliefs call us to work for justice and offer peace to a hurting world. Each chapter also offers reflection questions. As we strive to integrate these conversations into every aspect of our life, it is our hope that these resources might enable entire congregations to engage in meaningful conversations about justice that move us to faithful action.

When we listen to and learn from one another, we build bridges of understanding that can change the landscape of our communities and our world, as well as the geography of our own heart.

Reflection Questions

- Which stories from your own sacred texts and religious tradition have shaped your understanding of justice and service? What lessons and themes within those stories make them meaningful and memorable?

- Why does this book interest you? What do you hope to learn or gain from reading it?

- Would you go (or have you gone) to a worship service of another religion, different from your own? How would (or did) you feel about such an experience?

- Sometimes we have to look outside of our own religious tradition to gain inspiration. How have other religions inspired you? How have they enriched your work for justice?

- Have you heard or read any stories in the news this week about religion, or references in the news to a particular religious group? How did the news portray religion in these stories?

Care for the Environment

Diane's Introduction

I love to hike. When I am out in the woods, surrounded by the beauty and intricate diversity of nature, I feel an overwhelming sense of awe and peace. Standing on a remote mountain top or beside a babbling creek, my natural reaction is immense gratitude to the creator. In a world with so much competition and striving for success, multitudes of amazing creatures exist without the need for human effort or technology. And yet, the survival of these creatures is affected by the actions and decisions of humanity.

In the Christian creation story, God makes humans in the image of the divine and then gives them responsibility for all living things on the earth (Genesis 1:27–28). God brings the plants, animals, and celestial bodies into being and declares each of them good. Being formed in the likeness of the creator means humanity has not only the awesome ability of creativity but also the ability to delight in what has been made and to maintain its goodness.

Muslims, too, are taught to preserve and appreciate the gifts of creation. The Qur'an declares, "It is (Allah) Who hath made you (His) agents, inheritors of the earth" (6:165, Yusuf Ali) and reminds people that Allah does not love those who are wasteful (6:141, Yusuf Ali). Perhaps as a faith whose earliest followers lived in a dry and arid climate, water was held in special esteem. In a Hadith believers are told not to waste water even if they are at a running stream (Sunan Ibn Mājah 425).

Countless instructions in the Jewish Torah focus on caring for the earth and preventing waste. Sabbath and Jubilee, recurring times of rest mandated by Yahweh, were instituted not only for humans to enjoy a break from labor, but for the creatures and the land to experience a time of renewal as well. There's a delightful Jewish holiday called Tu B'Shevat, or new year of the trees, on which Jews are encouraged to enjoy a variety of fruits and nuts, in order to appreciate and learn from the bounty of God's gifts in creation.

The first precept of Buddhism is to refrain from taking life. Both Buddhists and Hindus seek to avoid causing harm or suffering to other living creatures, and many practice vegetarianism for this reason. While living in Sri Lanka, I was surprised when a Hindu friend refused to help me kill a family of giant cockroaches that had invaded my bathroom because it was an especially holy day on which she was committed to respecting the life of all beings— even roaches!

Our well-being, both physical and spiritual, is intimately connected to the well-being of our planet and all of its creatures. The responsibility to care for all of creation, and our obligation to respect and enjoy it, is central to the practice of nearly every faith tradition.

♍☪✡ॐ☧✝☾

Katy VanDusen has focused her efforts the past 37 years on education, spiritual growth, sustainability, and conservation in Costa Rica. In 1981, she led a diversification study that launched a successful artisan's cooperative and in 1988 published a book by and for campesinos in northwest Costa Rica about what they produce for home consumption. She coordinates the Monteverde Commission for Resilience to Climate Change (CORCLIMA). She has served on the board of directors of many conservation and education non-profits and as clerk of the Monteverde Friends Meeting, a Quaker (Christian) congregation. She also teaches yoga.

Faith, Practice, and Our Parking Lot

Sweat soaked my shirt under my armpits. Could those on the bench next to me feel my trembling? Was I quaking because I was moved by the Spirit? or by stubbornness?

We Quakers worship in silence, listening for that of God within. Similarly, when we make administrative decisions during our Monthly Meeting for Business, we listen for what the Spirit is asking of us. This requires open hearts and deep listening. Now, was I truly staying open?

Next on the agenda was a request from the Parking Lot Safety Committee to consider enlarging our parking lot, shared with the school. As the previous clerk of our Quaker Meeting, I had delayed bringing this topic for decision. I had urged the committee to focus on helping the community reduce incoming traffic and, more importantly, our greenhouse gas emissions, rather than expanding the lot. Unfortunately, that help hadn't come.

William, a school administrator, spoke. "Our parking lot is still not safe. Children are often almost hit by cars. Without action, there will be a tragedy."

We paused in silence. My heart beat faster.

Emily, a founding member of our community, stood to speak. In 1950, she, her husband, and 11 other Quaker families left the increasingly militarized United States for Costa Rica, which had just abolished its army. They founded Monteverde, which became the core of the largest block of privately conserved land in Costa Rica. "We used to have just grass, no parking lot," Emily said. "We lived nearby and walked. Now I come to meeting in a car. I understand the need for change."

I took several deep breaths and rose to speak. "The Carbon Neutrality Committee has calculated that over 90 percent of our emissions are from people driving here. Transport is also the biggest source of emissions in Costa Rica. The number of cars in the country has doubled in the last ten years. Our parking lot has become unsafe because there are too many cars. We could make the parking lot safe *and* reduce our carbon footprint by 75 percent if we had a school bus."

Silence.

I worked to listen openly when Chris stood. "The School Committee and parents reviewed a bus plan. The plan was met with resistance and the committee decided that it was not a priority for now. The costs and logistics of bus transport are complicated."

Not a priority for now? How could they say that while the Antarctic Peninsula is breaking apart; the Great Barrier Reef is dying; droughts in Syria, Somalia, and South Sudan are fueling famine and wars; and our cloud forest is drying up? Climate change is probably irreversible. It threatens the future safety of whole regions, especially poor regions. Quakers are supposed to walk the talk of stewardship. If we won't act on climate change, who will?

Stephanie stood up. "When I raised the question of ride-sharing, my neighbors told me that we need to 'respect our differences.' I tried to organize a van for students. That didn't work. And what about Meeting attenders taking responsibility for their emissions? Most don't just drive, they fly in airplanes!"

The knot in my stomach rose to my throat. She was speaking to my condition. I drive an electric golf cart locally, with almost no emissions since Costa Rica's electricity is 95 percent renewable, but I fly way too much. My family, including my 88-year-old mother, is in the United States. Could those of us who fly offset our footprint by supporting collective transport for students? But compensating wouldn't be enough. I would have to decline my husband's invitation for a trip to Alaska.

Chris stood again. "I suggest that we slow down, invite Spirit into our discussion, and be open to the possibilities."

Slow down? According to the Costa Rican who led the COP21 Paris talks, we're already ten years too late.

"I'd like to see efforts to improve the parking lot and the public bus system, and to create an electric bike-sharing program."

"My friends with electric bicycles are still addicted to their gas-guzzling cars," Harold said. "They want independence and convenience."

I asked the Light within for guidance on how to listen to the Divine in my fellow Friends whose proposal and slow response would inflict violence on the planet and its people. Ultimately, our clerk suggested we needed more time for discernment.

We settled again into silence, but my mind was active. Since my children left home, I found myself asking, "What am I called to do? How can I best use the next years of my life?" Perhaps I needed to move beyond my faith community by taking this climate mitigation work to the regional level. Was this the Spirit calling me?

☙❀✿☸✡✝☪

Fathimath Shafa is a senior at Westminster College in Fulton, Missouri. She is majoring in Biochemistry. After graduation she plans to take a gap year and then attend medical school. She holds a deep love for her people and her homeland, the Maldives.

Following My God and Caring for My Home: Reflections on Islands and Islam

I grew up in the Maldives, a South Asian island country, southwest of Sri Lanka and India. The Maldives is a country of islands and a country of Islam. Our location is in the middle of the Indian Ocean and we are a Muslim country. Our entire lifestyle focuses on existing in harmony with our environment and with our God. In school I studied Islam from an early age. What I didn't learn as a child was that our country itself was in danger. Our very livelihood, the land we live on, is under environmental threat.

Scientists predict that we will be the first climate refugees in the world. We're a small country, about 300,000 people, and the entire country is in danger of going under water completely. Our highest elevation above sea level is approximately five feet, meaning that as sea levels rise as a consequence of global warming, our islands will be submerged very quickly. There are no mountains, no places we are able to go as the waters increase. We are a small country without much power, and so while our government strives to address this environmental crisis, there is little we can do without help from the larger international community.

People in the Maldives know there are countries out there, people out there, who are doing more damage to the planet than we are. We do not have large centers of industry and we do not burn as much fossil fuel. We are doing less damage overall, compared to more powerful countries, yet the consequences we suffer will be dire. Even before the waters rise, even now, my country suffers. We are highly dependent on tourism and the fishing industry. These are our main sources of income, but because of environmental issues, carbon dioxide levels are high in the atmosphere, ultimately making the ocean water acidic, which in turn kills the fish. This impacts our fisherman. In addition, our underwater gardens, which are beautiful and unlike anything else in the world, attract a lot of tourists, but now the acidic ocean water is bleaching the corals and fewer and fewer tourists are coming to see them. The threat is already upon us. The consequences are already real.

Because we are Muslim, and because I grew up learning the teachings of the Prophet Muhammed, I know that care for creation and the environment are important. Hadith teaches us, "There is none amongst the Muslims who plants a tree or sows seeds, and then a bird, or a person or an animal eats from it, but is regarded as a charitable gift from him" (Sahih al-Bukhari 2320). In Islam planting trees, caring for creation, is an act of charity, and our faith calls us to acts of creation care.

The Qur'an teaches that all creatures are created in order to build a sense of community, so we must take care of one another. Nature is created to be interrelated. As Muslims we are called to be in relationship with one another and with creation and to make sure that we do not alter the creations of God. The Qur'an also instructs us to keep nature the way it was created. Otherwise, it's nearly impossible for God's people to return it to its original state. In the Maldives, we can see it even now, the damage the world has done. The polar ice caps are already melting; the sea levels are rising; my people and my home are suffering.

Many people assume that Islam is a religion of violence, that it teaches Muslims to hate and destroy. This is simply not the case. Islam is a faith that calls us to care for our fellow human beings and instructs us to live in peace with one another and with creation. It is a beautiful religion that has taught me so many things: to be a better person day by day, to love and live in peace, and to be thoughtful. My faith teaches me to care for my people, my country, and the world. My great hope is that others will join me in this work—that Buddhists, Muslims, Hindus, Jews, Atheists and Christians will all be able to see that we are all working toward the same goal—to save our planet and thus save creation for all those who come after us.

ॐ☯✡☾✵✝☪

Lindsey Bressler *cares about sustainable development and strong Jewish-Muslim relations. She is a senior at Northeastern University, majoring in International Affairs and Economics. Lindsey's spirituality has been influenced by her Jewish communities in Tucson, Arizona, and the Moishe Kavod House in Boston. Lindsey has completed internships at the Environmental Protection Agency, the Poverty Action Lab, and the Arava Institute for Environmental Studies in Israel. In her free time, Lindsey likes to pick up a good cup of black coffee, go for a run in the desert, or learn a new song on the ukulele.*

Finding Jewish Faith in the Soil

For much of college I believed that the spiritual foundation of my commitment to climate action was not my Jewish heritage but my newfound appreciation for Hinduism. I spent three summers in India and learned about the concept of multiple paths. In Hinduism, there is the idea that spirituality is a mountain leading to God. Although people can choose to travel different journeys to the top, there is still the same end. It is why, in Hinduism, there is tolerance for a variety of different forms of worship, different gods, and different rituals.

On my personal journey, I learned multiple paths to caring about climate action and multiple paths to being covered in sweat. As for what I learned about sweat, I have defined three categories. The first is the type that bubbles up on the sides of your nose in the middle of eating a spicy *dosa*, unexpected and sudden. Then there is the classic, more obvious kind of sweat that emerges from the intersection of humidity and long skirts. Perhaps most importantly, I experienced waves of sweat while sitting on a boat in the middle of the Ganges River at five in the morning. Watching the sunrise, sleep deprived, my body did not know what to do but to perspire, a third path to a damp body.

On that river I realized how deeply I cared about climate change. The Ganges, which winds through the Northeastern states in

India, is ascribed supreme spiritual significance. You can go to Varanasi to watch the dead be cremated, their ashes dumped into enormous funeral pyres on its banks. You can also track the Ganges River not by its religious sites but by its pollution. Going to the river and being in India incontrovertibly showed that the changes happening as a result of anthropogenic pollution were inordinately about humanness. I went to the river and I saw a way of life, a religious practice, a landscape being altered by pollution and rising temperatures and dwindling resources.

When I decided to spend a month farming as a part of a multi-faith institute for Jews, Muslims, and Christians, I was not able to understand how my Jewishness and my love for the earth lined up with each other. In an abstract sense, Judaism is linked to environmentalism. The holiday of Sukkot marks the joy of the harvest. Jews celebrate Sukkot by erecting a temporary outdoor structure with a leafy roof to see the stars. Another holiday, Tu B'Shevat, is entirely about trees. I remember donating my leftover change to charities that promised someone, somewhere would plant trees.

Even with these traditions in mind, I believed that Judaism and loving the earth came separately. In my heart, there were two types of people: strong, suntanned people, who camped and made compost piles in their backyards and had ancestors with green thumbs. These were a separate species from my people, who breathed in Bronx traffic fumes and were afraid of bugs.

At the farm, in a presentation on the basics of Islam, a wise Sufi woman shared that the word "religion" is based on the Latin root word *ligio,* which means to connect. In any type of religion, we strive to form links. Now I see that I care about the environment because I am Jewish and not in spite of it. Loving the earth and working to mitigate climate change is essential to living out a full spiritual practice.

While at the farm, I picked up a copy of *Scripture, Culture and Agriculture: An Agrarian Reading of the Bible*[1] by Old Testament scholar Ellen F. Davis. In the book, I found a new meaning to liturgical passages. I realized that the Torah, a document I had so long felt

---

[1]Ellen F. Davis, *Scripture, Culture and Agriculture: An Agrarian Reading of the Bible* (Cambridge: Cambridge University Press, 2009).

not relevant to me, provided a strong validation for an ethic of land care and climate justice. For instance, the biblical practice of giving agricultural land a Sabbath rest shows that humanity has a need to care for and show reverence for natural forces.

It was not until I got my fingernails dirty that I learned that faith—Jewish faith—is in the soil just as naturally as it is a part of my people and my text. Although my grandparents may not have been farmers, I know that pursuing a more environmentally just world is rooted in who I am and not something that I have to look entirely outside of my heritage to find.

✿☯☸ॐ☫✝☾

Todd Fields and his wife have been involved with the Raleigh Mennonite Church for most of their 43 years of marriage, but he became interested in yoga and Buddhism about 15 years ago. That interest led him to become a certified yoga teacher and an ordained Buddhist minister in the tradition of the Vietnamese Zen master Thich Nhat Hanh. Today he is mostly retired from a remodeling contracting career, lives in Raleigh, and relates to The Community for Mindful Living UUFR (Thich Nhat Hanh tradition), Won Buddhism of NC (Korean tradition), Moving Mantra Yoga, and the Raleigh Mennonite Church.

What the Buddha Showed Me about Mother Earth

In the post-1960s era, I was studying and practicing Christianity whole-heartedly. I had been influenced deeply by the socio-political movements of the day, particularly by growing awareness of "the environment." In 1973 I took Ecology 101 at the University of North Carolina. I believe it was one of the first college ecology courses ever taught. I built a passive solar house, composted my waste, did some vegetable gardening, and heated with wood when the sun wasn't enough. You could say I was an environmentalist, but I was not a "tree hugger." My concern for the environment did not have a spiritual component.

Around the age of 50 I began to encounter the teachings of the Buddha. It could be said that the Buddha was the first environmentalist, but his view was a little different from what we normally think. We tend to think of the environment as all the stuff around us. The Buddha taught that we are not separate from the environment. We actually *are* the environment. Our bodies are made of minerals from the soil, moisture from the clouds, oxygen from the atmosphere, and energy from the sun. Even our emotional, mental, and spiritual selves cannot be separated from that of our parents, friends, and society. Zen master Thich Nhat Hanh coined the term "inter-being" to describe this reality. We all "inter-are" with everything and everyone on the earth.

In meditation or when walking in the woods I am sometimes able to touch this truth in a deep way, and this realization inspires a feeling of understanding, love, and compassion. I have the feeling that the earth really is my mother. The term "Mother Earth" is no longer just a quaint phrase. She has created me. Her DNA is in every cell of my body. With every breath, every bite of broccoli, she sustains me. I begin to feel that I am in love with Mother Earth. Sometimes I actually do go and hug a tree. I put my arms around it, my cheek up against the bark, and I offer gratitude for the oxygen she supplies. In this way my environmentalism becomes very deep and spiritual.

Many Christians believe in a Kingdom of Heaven. We may think of this as a place far away, filled with beauty and inhabited by saints, where we may be able to go in the future. Many Buddhists also imagine a Pure Land of the Buddha, which is said to lie far to the west, and to be full of flowers, songbirds, and many Buddhas and bodhisattvas (any being who has completely devoted herself to ending the suffering of others). Pure Land Buddhists believe if they recite the name of the Buddha many times and keep the precepts, they may one day be reborn in the Pure Land. Perhaps there is some truth to these visions, but Zen Buddhism also teaches that the Pure Land of the Buddha is actually here and now. This magnificent, beautiful earth is our mother, our refuge, our sustainer. This is it. There is no place else to go. Whether our environment is heaven or hell depends on us. The Pure Land is not a place, organization, government, or church. A Pure Land is anywhere there is beauty, understanding, compassion, joy, and equanimity.

In Christianity we generally think there is only one Kingdom of God, but in Buddhism there can be many Pure Lands of the Buddha, because there are many Buddhas. Jesus was the Son of God, very holy and unique; but from a Buddhist point of view, who is not a child of God? Each of us is a Buddha-to-be. We only need to open our hearts to the Holy Spirit. With the Holy Spirit we can each create a Pure Land for ourselves and the world around us by living with mindfulness and compassion in each moment. With each breath, each step, each word and action we manifest our love for God, for Mother Earth, and for all her children. In this way we become true environmentalists.

Our planet is in a dire situation. Many species are becoming extinct. The warming of the atmosphere is causing irreversible changes. Our air, water, and soil are increasingly polluted. In a hundred or two hundred years it may not be possible for humans to live on the earth. All of this has been caused by our lack of understanding, greed, and selfishness; but I don't think becoming an angry, panicked activist is the answer. In this critical moment in human history I believe that what is needed more than ever is the energy of love, peace, and wisdom. I am thankful for Jesus' teachings about this spirit, and I am thankful for the ways in which my Buddhist training has given me tools to manifest healing in myself and in the world.

ॐ☬✡☸☯✝☪

Sarah Franklin *is a Celtic-Pagan who works to build bridges between religious communities and educates people about Paganism to dispel myths and fears. She has spoken at interfaith events at the University of Alabama at Birmingham, where she currently works in the School of Public Health. Sarah runs a religious organization for Pagan, Wiccan, and other earth-based faith students at UAB. She earned her degree in Public Health and has conducted and collaborated on studies examining Hepatitis B, HIV, maternal and child health, and non-communicable diseases. She has co-authored multiple research papers.*

Return to the Earth

Imagine this: *When the earth was created, there was no time and no gods, and no man walked the surface of the land. But there was the sea, and where the sea met the land, a mare was born, white and made from the sea-foam. Her name was Eiocha, and from an oak tree that grew in the land there sprouted a plant. This is where Eiocha gave birth to the first god Cernunnos, who then mated with Eiocha and created more gods; however, the gods felt lonely and wanted to be adored, so from the wood of the oak tree they created the first people as well as other animals. Giants, too, are born from the bark of a tree that Eiocha hurled into the water.*

This particular story is from Celtic legends and is one of many creation stories in ancient mythologies across the globe. It shows the deep connection that our gods have with the universe. The gods and goddesses are not just the creators of the planet, but they were brought up from the trees, ocean, and sky themselves. They did not create the earth, but instead they are one with the earth. Being a Pagan means that our religion is almost completely enmeshed with nature and her beauty. The gods assigned themselves roles according to what they look after in the universe, making themselves gods of the sky, oceans, earth, trees, rain, sun, and every other aspect of the natural world. Most Pagans, including myself, feel obligated to protect and preserve the world around us because it contains the essence of our gods and is our home. The planet Earth is often referred to as a feminine force or a goddess; even in modern-day terms we call her Mother Nature or Mother Earth. To Pagans the earth is our mother, and we belong to the universe. The other animals on the planet are my family. My pets are not my property but my brothers and sisters. As a Pagan, I feel the spirits of my loved ones in the wind, trees, and my surroundings.

Pagans believe all of nature is connected, from the largest tree to the smallest worm. Pagans try to respect life on earth and do not kill other creatures unless necessary to eat. Killing for sport is largely viewed as disgraceful, as is wasting life for the sheer joy of killing. Because I am a Pagan, I am also a vegetarian and an animal-rights activist. I chose to stop eating meat because I could not bear the idea of my brothers and sisters suffering for my pleasure when I could easily relieve their suffering.

With climate change and the ice caps melting, many species are losing their homes, causing deterioration or extinction. To me, helping the planet and others is an act of worship; when I see a little animal in the road and I stop to help it cross, I say a prayer and ask the goddess of animals to keep this creature safe.

The planet and its resources can replenish and heal over time, but it is evident that the resources we require are being used up at a rate that the planet has never seen before. I fear we will bring about the destruction of our own species, yet I am comforted by the idea that the human race may come to an end and leave behind other creatures to recover and exist comfortably. I think the biggest conflict I have come across with other people is the belief that a deity would not let the earth and humans be destroyed; however, we cannot deny the evidence that is literally in front of our eyes. I think most Pagans differ from other religions in that we do not consider ourselves the gods' greatest creation. We know that the gods would let our own species die off so that the earth could heal and other species could be saved. I feel that we as a human race have no sense of self-preservation and will destroy ourselves as well as the environment around us, so maybe it is a good thing that our species could eventually become extinct. The planet could exist perfectly without us. Mother Earth will recover, but we will not. We are not destroying the planet; we are destroying ourselves and taking others down with us. I believe the key point right now would be just to try to preserve what we have left. If we do not change our habits and consumption, there will no longer be a human race. The planet and the ecosystems can evolve to fit the changing world, but we might not be able to exist in the changing environment.

Reflection Questions

- Lindsey Bressler discovers resources within her Jewish tradition that encourage care for the earth. What holy texts, stories, or traditions in your own religious or spiritual background foster concern for environmental justice?

- Katy VanDusen writes of listening to the Spirit's call for her to stand up and do more about climate change, beyond a faith community that does not share her sense of urgency. Have you felt frustrated by your faith community's response to calls for justice? How has that impacted your faith? How have you been moved to respond? What are some ways you would like to work for change within your faith community?

- The Quaker tradition relies on silence and listening in its worship and decision-making. What practices help you in both your spiritual life and your work for justice?

- The Qur'an calls for all creatures to exist in interconnected community with one another. How does your religious or spiritual background teach you to relate to other living beings, beyond humans? How do you view the connection between your actions and the well-being of others whom you may not even meet, such as people who live in the Maldives? Do you believe you have a responsibility to them, and if so, in what way?

- How do you believe the world and everything in it came to be? Does your religion have a creation story or an origin story? How does your understanding of the earth's origins impact your sense of responsibility to care for the earth?

- Sarah Franklin sees helping the planet as an act of worship. Do you view your justice work as a form of worship?

Race and Privilege

Jamie Lynn's Introduction

#BlackLivesMatter

This hashtag was initially written in a Facebook post by Alicia Garza following the acquittal of George Zimmerman on July 13, 2013. Zimmerman shot and killed Trayvon Martin, a seventeen-year-old African American, on February 26, 2012. The hashtag #BlackLivesMatter then became a movement led by three women: Alicia Garza, Opal Tometi, and Patrisse Cullors. They define the movement as "...an ideological and political intervention in a world where Black lives are systematically and intentionally targeted for demise. It is an affirmation of Black folks' contributions to this society, our humanity, and our resilience in the face of deadly oppression."[1]

"Hands up, don't shoot."

This phrase was uttered by protesters in the days and weeks following the August 9, 2014, death of Michael Brown, an eighteen-year-old African American, at the hands of a white police officer in Ferguson, Missouri. With a string of deaths that included Martin and Brown, the mainstream media began to take note of the

---

[1]See http://blacklivesmatter.com/herstory/.

violence impacting black lives at the hands of authorities. Names like Eric Garner (who was killed in July, prior to Brown), Sandra Bland, Tamir Rice, Walter Scott, and Freddie Gray began to enter our cultural consciousness.

Progressive communities of faith began to ask how they were being called to respond. In Ferguson, faith leaders from Christian, Muslim, Buddhist, and Jewish communities—among many others—stood with protesters, kneeled in front of police officers, and offered prayer. They interrupted traffic as a form of protest, and churches held community meetings in an attempt to hold city leaders accountable. Houses of worship across the city of St. Louis and across the country hung "Black Lives Matter" banners as a form of witness. State-sponsored violence against people of color has unfolded since before our country's founding, and religious communities again find themselves faced with the question of how they are called to faithfully respond.

When Michael Brown was shot, I was co-teaching a semester-long Religious Studies course called *Prophetic Leadership for Systemic Change*. Westminster College, where I served as chaplain at the time, is located 90 minutes from Ferguson, and our students felt the energy, unrest, and the call for justice unfolding in the city. During one class a student from Ferguson raised her hand to interrupt a more academic, theoretical conversation and said, "Jamie, I hear you talking about all this theology stuff, using big words and quoting fancy books, but what I really want to know is, what would Jesus do if he lived in Ferguson?" Her question immediately struck me as important, at the very heart of the matter. What would Jesus do?

We know Jesus spoke up and spoke out against injustice—he healed; he loved; he protested against the violence of Roman authorities, and because of this protest, he lost his life. "I think Jesus would be there, protesting, every day and every night," I said.

Christianity calls us to work toward racial reconciliation, as do many other faith traditions. The Prophet Muhammed, in his final speech, reminded Muslims that only good actions and devotion to God made one person more worthy of admiration than another. Uniting people around their highest values, rather than their differences, is central to many religions.

✿✤✳︎ॐ✧✝☾

Eiman Ali is a Somali-American Muslim living in Raleigh, North Carolina. She is passionate about social justice and co-founded a Raleigh-based non-profit called Muslim Women For, which is a Muslim women–led social justice organization. She graduated from Meredith College with a degree in Biology and a minor in Public Health, and is pursuing a career in clinical research. She loves road tripping, playing the ukulele, reading, and watching movies with her brothers and sisters.

One Ummah, Under God

Sunday school classes were a big part of my childhood. While my parents enrolled me in public school, they made sure I was always part of an Islamic school, which my Somali family called a *duugsi,* on weekends or weekday evenings. It was important to my parents that I learned about my faith and its history. I made many Muslim friends because of this, which is fortunate because Muslims didn't seem to exist in my life outside of that. In public school, I was one of many students of color, but not many shared my religion. In Sunday school, I was one of many Muslims, but not many shared my dark complexion. Being able to have a space to explore both identities was beneficial, but not having a space where the two intersections were shared proved to be detrimental in ways I didn't realize until years later.

One day in my Islamic class of predominantly South Asians and Arabs, I walked in to see a substitute. I rejoiced with my peers because this sub was a young man and because he didn't have a thick accent like most of our teachers. Today was clearly going to be a "chill" day. Only a few minutes into the class, the room was filled with chatter. I was ten years old and at this age, it was typical of classrooms to be split down the middle by an invisible barrier, separating boys and girls. The sub hung with the boys while I scooched up to my best friend. Suddenly, I heard something that made my heart sink: "I would never marry a girl darker than me!"

I scanned for the source of the voice. It was none other than the substitute teacher. He was standing in front of the group of young boys, laughing, and the boys shared in the amusement with shy, stifled laughter. I was humiliated to see that I was the only black girl in the room. I was also the darkest. The sub soon followed his disgusting statement with "unless it was Beyoncé, of course!"

I could feel my face grow hot. Even as a ten-year-old, I was aware of the anti-blackness that poisoned these spaces. Even darker-skinned South Asians and Arabs felt the sting of colorism. I did everything in my power to fight it. I always stood up for myself. But in this moment, I felt completely powerless. This was an adult man, the appointed leader of the class, casually spreading his misogyny and anti-blackness to impressionable boys, and there was nothing I could do about it. The day had turned completely sour.

Colorism is a reality I had been introduced to at a young age. It ravages most communities, even predominantly black ones like my own. My parents instilled in me that who I am as a person is more important than anything, but also made sure I felt just as beautiful on the outside. And I did. I was a proud little girl, always telling people about my identities as a black, African Muslima. So when I heard such comments, it cut me deep, not because I was feeling insecure, but because I was reminded that the world may never see me the way I see myself.

This is a struggle I have dealt with my whole life, in both Muslim and non-Muslim spaces. Discrimination against darker-skinned people is not unique to Muslim-majority cultures. It was the imperialism and colonization of Europeans that brought white supremacy to the rest of the world, after all. However, I hold my *ummah,* or global Muslim community, to a high standard because our shared values adamantly state that race and culture should never divide us. I often go back to a hadith, which is a record of sayings and traditions of the Prophet Muhammed (peace be upon him), where he stated, "There is no superiority for an Arab over a non-Arab, nor for a non-Arab over an Arab. Neither is the white superior over the black, nor is the black superior over the white—except by piety." Islamic history is full of black figures who were crucial for the way the religion is practiced today. This verse in Surah Al-Hujurat celebrates our differences: "O mankind, indeed We have created you from male and female and made you peoples and tribes that you may know one another. Indeed, the most noble of you in the sight of Allah is the most righteous of you.

Indeed, Allah is Knowing and Acquainted" (49:13, Sahih). It is not enough to be made up of different races, features, languages, and cultural traditions. We must engage with one another and show one another the love and respect we expect from all, Muslims or non-Muslims alike.

ॐ☬☪۩✡☥✝☾

Samuel Voth Schrag *served as the pastor of the St. Louis Mennonite Fellowship from 2007–2017, and also served on the board of Mennonite Church USA and Community Mediation Services of St. Louis. He co-chaired the clergy caucus of Metropolitan Congregations United. He is from Wichita, Kansas, and is a graduate of Bethel College (Kansas) and the Anabaptist Mennonite Biblical Seminary. He is married to Rachel and has two children, Jonah and Hannah.*

An Accidental Protestor

I never expected to be a protestor.

I am a Mennonite pastor, and Mennonites have a tradition of being the "quiet in the land"—a community most concerned about being good citizens, not rocking the boat. Many Mennonites have even chosen not to vote as a way of separating themselves from the work of the government. If we are going to protest, it's usually in an anti-war movement, calling for the peace of Christ to dwell more deliberately in the world.

Nevertheless, I found myself on the streets of Ferguson in the fall of 2014, after Michael Brown had been killed, joining with protestors calling for a different way of doing law enforcement in America, proclaiming that Black Lives Matter.

It's been a stretching experience. I've gone outside my comfort zone, helping organize marches, watching friends get arrested, chanting slogans, and asking my congregation to go outside their comfort zone as well. It would have been easy to take the route of leaving the politics to the politicians, not to cause trouble.

But as a follower of Jesus, I found myself drawn into the work of anti-racism in St. Louis. After all, racism is one of the founding sins of America. This is a nation built on slave labor and the theft of land from Native Americans. The Bible's liberation narrative—the Hebrew people escaping Egypt, struggling for freedom from foreign empires, and praying for freedom from Rome—calls us to examine our history. If, as the prophet Isaiah foretold, people are coming from the east and the west to feast at the table of God, there is work we need to do to get our communities to look a little more like God's kingdom.

Jesus was always on the margins, hanging out with sinners and tax collectors, listening to John the Baptist's wild sermons, arguing with the Pharisees. In the case of unarmed people standing before the massive paramilitary apparatus of the state, I believe that Jesus has to be hanging out with those on the streets. So, I went out to the streets—sometimes with thousands of other protestors, blocking traffic and asking for attention; sometimes with just a few, keeping lonely vigil across from the Ferguson police department.

Once I started hanging out with protestors, I found myself drawn to their stories. I couldn't stay on my old path. I saw many predominantly white churches ignore what was happening, never letting it shape their ministry. But I couldn't stay silent while my friends were struggling for liberation. To claim an apolitical stance is to side with the status quo, with those in power who like things the way they are.

I have heard nasty language used about protestors: "thugs," "gang bangers," "outside instigators." After being in Ferguson late at night, with crowds of protestors across from police in riot gear, I knew that these weren't thugs, but children of God asking to be policed in a different way, asking that their bodies be treated with the same respect as mine. Before I became a protestor, I knew that our country incarcerated black men at six times the rate of white men, and had created urban environments that perpetuate a cycle of violence and poverty, but on the streets I heard stories of what this looked like in practice.

I have heard again and again "All Lives Matter" as a response to Black Lives Matter. Of course, all lives do matter. But I have a deeper sense now of how hurtful it is to respond to "Black Lives Matter" with "All Lives Matter." It is to respond to "Blessed are the poor in Spirit" with "Everyone's Blessed." In St. Louis, in zip codes just a few miles away, the life expectancy drops by 18 years when going from a largely white, well-to-do community to a nearly entirely poor, black community. Our nation has said historically, and today, that black lives matter *less*. We must do better.

So I've been doing what I can. We, and I, could all do more. I know the nights I didn't go out. The times other agendas took me away, or when I was anxious and chose not to make waves. I know the people I look to who have done more than me, who have more fully incorporated anti-racism into their lives and their ministry. I don't think it's useful to let guilt drive us. Instead, I hope you think about another step you might take. A letter you might write. A church service you might visit. A question you might ask. A march you might join. There is work to be done, and you are able to do it.

ॐ☬✡ॐ☯✝☪

Rabbi Lucy Dinner *has served Temple Beth Or in Raleigh, North Carolina, as Senior Rabbi since 1993. She graduated from the University of North Carolina–Chapel Hill with a degree in Public Policy Analysis, and was ordained at the Hebrew Union College–Jewish Institute of Religion in Cincinnati, Ohio. Her writing has been published in Women's Torah Commentary. Rabbi Dinner is the Chair of the Central Conference of American Rabbis' Peace and Justice Committee and Vice Chair of the Union for Reform Judaism's Commission on Social Action. In 2016, Rabbi Dinner received the NAACP North Carolina Religious Leadership Award. Rabbi Dinner and her husband have two sons, and two grandchildren.*

Who's Going to Believe This?

I grew up in New Orleans at the tail end of the civil rights movement, when racial issues were still very raw. The Ku Klux Klan was very active. David Duke's childhood home was literally down the block from where I grew up. The Klan was so open about their activities that I have memories of the KKK giving out leaflets at stoplights. They didn't have masks over their faces, but they were dressed in KKK garb. It was very public, and meant to be intimidating.

When I was in high school, I went with a friend to a KKK bookstore to do a report for social studies. All kinds of pamphlets lined the shelves of the small storefront: antisemitic, anti-black, anti-Mexican. The vehement, raw hatred of the publications shocked me, as a young Jew. I knew the KKK was antisemitic, but I had no idea of the depth of their hatred against Jews. Two-thirds of the pamphlets focused on spewing revulsion of Jews. They glorified *The Protocols of Zion,* celebrated the death of Jews in the Holocaust, and were filled with demonized drawings of Jews. They fed age-old antisemitic falsehoods ranging from "Jews caused the plague" to "Jews own the media, Hollywood, and Congress." The blatant exaggeration and clear fabrications of hate did not initially worry me. As an intellectual teenager I thought that any rational person would clearly see through these lies: "Who's going to believe this?"

Twenty minutes into our explorations in the bookstore, there was a knock on the door and a seven- or eight-year-old boy walked in. He was the son of the person working there. My friend and I looked at each other and said, "That's who is going to believe this." That moment brought me to the crushing realization that anyone who grows up with parents feeding them hatred alongside their breakfast cereal will know hatred as their primary worldview.

That pivotal moment in the KKK bookstore transformed my own naïve worldview. The unfiltered hatred that permeated the store sealed my commitment to combating prejudice. In that moment the prophetic teachings of my Jewish tradition—to love mercy, to do justly, and to walk humbly with God—solidified as my mission to eradicate hatred.

The resurgence of xenophobia today is no surprise, given the glorification of prejudice across all forms of communication in our culture. The truth no longer matters as much as the attention-grabbing sound bite. Now more than ever, I feel urgency to speak out against oppression in all its forms. Today, in both my professional and personal life, I keep justice at the center of my passions. I continue to serve on boards and committees that focus on social action.

More than ever, we need to join with people of all faiths and beyond to eradicate the hate and oppression that permeates society. In the past decade Jews have particularly joined our justice work with that of people of color. We see the systemic oppression of blacks and other people of color as an affront to democracy and humanity. The 1964 Civil Rights Act was written in the building that now serves as the office of the Religious Action Center for Reform Judaism. Kivie Kaplan, a Reform Jew, was president of the NAACP and presided as the Civil Rights Act came into fruition. The irony of gathering to eradicate hatred today, in that same space where the Civil Rights Act was written, is a chilling reminder of the need to pursue justice in every generation.

Thirty-six times the Hebrew Bible says, "You shall not oppress the stranger, for you were strangers in the land of Egypt." Thirty-six is a special number in Hebrew tradition because it is a symbol of life. Our lives and the vitality of the world depend on how we treat one another—the value we place on every person, even the stranger. This universal commandment to stand up for the oppressed, to elevate life, supersedes all other commitments in Judaism

Judaism offers a particular path for Jews, in ritual and faith, to approach God. That path is complemented by the universal command to unite with all humanity in bringing healing to the world. Our faith teaches that the Jewish path is but one of many particular paths that shape the way people see themselves before God. Our task is to join together with those across all faiths and cultures in the quest for a better world. Judaism offers one way to ascend the mountain. Christianity and Islam share their particular paths, and scores of others march path by path, step by step, up the mountain to build a world that respects all humanity.

⚘☸✡☦✝☪

Jem Jebbia *is a PhD student in Religious Studies at Stanford University. In her studies, Jem focuses on interfaith pedagogies, race and gender in interfaith communities, and material religion. Her current projects include an ethnographic study of college and university chaplains and a pop-up museum exhibit depicting the religious history of California. Jem also writes for several online publications and serves as a Writing Fellow for the Revolutionary Love Project.*

The Privilege to Play

When I was nine, I joined an all-Japanese American basketball team in Southern California. My best friend was Japanese American, and she invited me to join the Saberette Sunshooters. They needed another player (each team was allowed two non-Japanese players), and I happily signed up because I loved sports. My dad enthusiastically agreed to drive me to practice every Saturday and games every Sunday. Sometimes the games were hours away. Our practices were held at the East San Gabriel Valley Japanese Community Center—the place where I would first learn about Buddhism, the faith I now call my own.

I was the only non-Japanese player on the team, and I towered over everyone. While I felt deeply aware that my skin and hair did not look like my teammates', I was ignorant of the power and privilege I carried as a young white woman. I wanted to prove I was just like them, so I tried everything—I dressed like them, ate the same foods, and took interest in what my teammates liked. My teammates and their families always welcomed me.

As a travel team, the Sunshooters played in tournaments all over California and Nevada. The first time we won a tournament against our rival team, our coaches took us out for a special treat: King's Hawaiian bread. Growing up with this team, I slowly learned what it might mean to be Japanese-American for my teammates, but I never grappled with being white.

In fifth grade, the Sunshooters were invited to play in a tournament hosted by the Enchantees, a non-profit organization in San Francisco dedicated to youth sports for Japanese Americans. The parents booked rooms at the Embassy Suites, and one big room for all ten of us girls. We stayed up all night before our first game, watching TV and playing truth or dare. The next day after we played our games, our parents could tell we were dragging. Despite the exhaustion, I remember feeling so happy to feel like part of this community. Basketball brought us together, but sharing our innermost secrets felt like true friendship.

Almost a year later, my dad started talking about the Enchantees tournament. He loved spending time with the other parents and watching the games. We waited to hear the dates of the tournament, until my dad finally asked Coach Kal if they had cancelled it. Kal's face turned red and he grew quiet. He shuffled his feet for a few moments before telling my dad why we wouldn't play in the tournament this year. "They are only allowing Japanese players," he mumbled. My dad and I talked about this on the way home. We agreed the team should go without us. "We can go and cheer your team on," dad assured me.

When my dad suggested this to Kal, he shook his head "no." "We are a family," he said. "We only play as one." We never returned to the Enchantees tournament.

It has been a long time since I played center for the Sunshooters, and over the past decade I have wrestled with my whiteness—how I was oblivious to privilege and attempted to assume a different identity. At the same time, the Buddhist ethics and practice that I have adopted for the last 15 years has allowed me to unpack and reflect on this incident, and on my presence on this basketball team. Being part of this team taught me about commitment to a community, and I deeply appreciate growing up with such an amazing group of young women. At the same time, I have worked through intense feelings of guilt around my whiteness and taking a space on a team that in no way owed me that space.

How do I reconcile guilt and reality? My faith teaches me first and foremost that every human being suffers, and my job is to help end the suffering of others. Knowing this, I also believe self-reflection serves me well to better understand how to end this suffering. Recognizing the privilege I have and will hold my entire life, embedded in my white skin—access to education, a stable family environment, and other pieces of my identity—helps me feel empowered to fight racism and religious intolerance, among other forms of bigotry. I make mistakes often, and I certainly do not consider myself an expert. At the same time, my meditation practice allows me to know the reality of the world around me and to not feel frozen in this messy, difficult work of dismantling systems of oppression. I carry the loyalty of my basketball team with me, knowing that if a community can show up for me like that, I can do the same for others who are suffering.

 ☸☪✡ॐ☥✝☾

Sulaiman Ahmad *is from Greenville, South Carolina. He attends Furman University, where he is majoring in Politics and International Affairs.*

What's in a Name?

I was born and raised in Greenville, South Carolina. As a Muslim American, growing up in the South has not been easy. In an effort to assimilate, I tried going by the nickname Sully. It sounded more American, and people remembered it because it was easier to pronounce. But even this nickname could not shield me from the bigotry that arose from the 2016 general election. It was my sophomore year of college, and I was part of Furman University's study-away program in Washington, D.C. I was living with three other guys in an apartment. One was a good friend from Furman, and the other two were students from the University of Rhode Island and the University of New Hampshire. These students also happened to be Trump supporters, so needless to say we had many political discussions during our time spent together. Even in the many debates we had, nothing hurt me as much as when one of the parents of my roommates acted purely out of Islamophobia. This parent asked his son what my name was, and upon finding out, he told his son that if I prayed five times a day I am a radical. He also told his son that they should put pork in the refrigerator to see what my reaction would be. I was wounded that someone would label me as a radical just because of my name.

That is when I remembered a story my mother told about Prophet Muhammad (peace be upon him). My mother told me that one day when the Prophet was walking down the street, a woman took her waste bin and poured refuse on the Prophet as he passed by her window. This would recur every day; however, the Prophet continued on with his day. One day as he passed by the same window, he noticed that nothing had been poured onto him. Surprised by this, he visited the woman and found out that she had fallen ill. He offered her assistance, and humbled by the Prophet's kindness she became ashamed of her actions. From that day forth, the woman understood the true meaning of Islam. This story is one that I have carried throughout my life. Despite all the hatred I have faced, I continue to strive forward and help those who need it. This is a difficult and lonely path, but it is the path of what Islam truly is.

I cannot blame my roommate's father for thinking what he did. The media has consistently perpetuated an image of Muslims as barbaric warmongers, which instills fear in people. This fear is exactly what I see projected onto me when people shout racial slurs or attack my faith. After the experience I had in Washington, D.C., I decided to stop calling myself "Sully." I realized that if my name, "Sulaiman," could cause such a disturbance, I should continue to go by that name. Muhammad Ali realized this when he stopped calling himself Cassius Clay. He said in an interview, "You wanna keep calling me a white man's name, I ain't white." That same epiphany struck me as I realized that I had watered down the powerful name Sulaiman to better assimilate myself. In Abrahamic religions, Sulaiman comes from the name Solomon, who was a king and a prophet. My faith guided me to be proud of my name and my religion, despite the struggles I may face in the future.

Reflection Questions

- What has been your personal experience with racism and privilege? Have you had encounters in which you were treated differently than others because of the color of your skin?

- What factors make up your identity? With what groups do you identify and feel most comfortable?

- Samuel Voth Schrag viewed himself as an unlikely protester. Are there teachings in your religious tradition that call followers to avoid engaging in political issues, or that are frequently cited to support non-involvement? Are there teachings in your religious tradition that call followers to advocate for change and to challenge unjust powers?

- Have you ever heard stereotypes or prejudices about a particular group of people (whether based on religion, race, ethnicity, or another classification) from leaders in your house of worship? Are such views supported in your religious community? How do you feel about such views?

- Are there stories or scriptures within your religion that celebrate diversity? Are there stories or scriptures that are used to argue that some races, ethnicities, nationalities, or cultural groups are superior to others? How are those texts interpreted and applied today? How have those texts been interpreted and applied in the past?

- What ideas or texts within your religion inspire you to stand up against racism? What resources or tools within your religion give you strength and hope to address such a complex problem?

Immigration and Refugees

Diane's Introduction

Offering hospitality to immigrants and refugees is both humbling and empowering. It can teach us how limited our own understanding and perspective is, and open us up to practicing selfless love and compassion in ways we might not have known possible.

In my own travels, I have experienced gracious hospitality that reaches across national and religious boundaries in powerful ways. As a Christian missionary and English teacher living in rural northern Sri Lanka, Hindu neighbors invited me into their home and treated me like one of their own daughters. While so much of what they practiced and believed felt foreign to me, they accepted me as I was, opened their home, and shared their food and their lives with me, creating a powerful sense of connection. Through their hospitality to me, a stranger, I felt at home.

I have also been privileged to welcome strangers and help them make a new home in the United States through my church, which has befriended many refugee families. Walking alongside our new neighbors as they adapt to a very different culture has opened our eyes to see our own country and faith in a new way. Reading scriptures alongside people whose life journey has been so different from mine, I gain fresh insights from their interpretation and their questions. Witnessing their gratitude for the freedom and safety they experience here renews my pride for this country's ideals and opportunities.

The foundational stories of many of the world's religions are stories of immigrants and refugees. Our sacred texts are full of people on the move—people seeking freedom and safety in a new land, people crossing borders to share their faith, people sent on a journey by God. Christianity, Islam, and Judaism share common ancestors, such as Abraham and Sarah, whom God called to set out for unknown lands, so that they could be a blessing to many; Hagar and Ishmael, whose cries God heard when they had to leave the safety of home and make their way through the wilderness; Moses and Miriam, who led the enslaved Israelites out of Egypt to freedom from Pharaoh's harsh oppression; and Jesus, whose family fled to Egypt after his birth to escape persecution by King Herod.

The early followers of Jesus, from the twelve disciples to the apostle Paul, constantly traveled to new places to teach and preach about their beliefs. The Buddha, too, spent much of his life as a traveling teacher. In many religious traditions, the faith was first passed on by people dependent on the hospitality of strangers.

The teaching to care for one's neighbor—found in nearly every religion's scriptures—transcends local geography and national borders. When Jesus offers the parable of the good Samaritan to illustrate what it means to love one's neighbor as one's self, his example concludes with the lesson that a neighbor is a person who treats someone in need with mercy. Hospitality for foreigners and the oppressed is a primary value emphasized across traditions.

The Hindu Taitiriya Upanishad teaches that guests are to be considered like God, in the same way that mothers, fathers, and teachers are (Taittiriya Upanishad 1.11.2). In the Christian New Testament, Jesus proclaims that when you welcome a stranger, it is like you welcome God (Matthew 25:31–46). Both the Jewish Torah and the Christian Old Testament instruct followers to love the foreigners living among them as they love themselves, because of their own history as foreigners residing in Egypt. According to the Qur'an, Muslims are to "do good unto your parents, and near of kin, and unto orphans and the needy, and the neighbor from among your own people, and the neighbor who is a stranger, and the friend by your side, and the wayfarer…" (4:36, Muhammad Asad). Buddhists aspire to treat others with compassion and lovingkindness, seeking to free people from their suffering. The Second Precept of Buddhism calls on followers to practice generosity and ensure that others' basic needs are met.[1] Over and over again, the faithful are taught that foreigners in need among us are to be shown the same compassion as our own family and friends.

☬☸✡︎✿✝︎☪︎

Maya Wahrman *started volunteering with immigrant and refugee neighbors in New Jersey while developing a program on religion and forced migration at Princeton University's Office of Religious Life. This inspiring work, and the friendships she built with detained asylum-seekers, local Central American high school students, and resettled refugees led her to pursue direct client service work for immigrants. She now works at the Latin American Legal Defense and Education Fund in Trenton, New Jersey, and is beginning a Masters of Social Work program at Rutgers. She hopes to continue writing essays and poetry as she begins this new chapter. Her previously published work is available at mayawahrman. com.*

God Is Everywhere

I met M from El Salvador when I was a weekly visitor to the Elizabeth Detention Center from 2016–2018, befriending imprisoned asylum seekers as they awaited trial. M was eventually deported, and after a few months we lost touch. I cannot say whether it was because he stopped being able to afford his phone bill or if he met a far worse fate. This open letter says so much of what I wish I could still share with him.

Querido M,

They taught me in Hebrew school that God is everywhere. You cannot see God, and God does not respond directly when you pray. But God is everywhere.

---

[1]Thich Nhat Hahn, *For a Future to Be Possible: Buddhist Ethics for Everyday Life,* rev. ed. (1993; Berkeley, Calif.: Parallax Press, 2007). See also https://www. esolibris.com/articles/buddhism/buddhism_precept_2.php .

When I was older, they taught us that all human beings are created *b'tzelem Elohim,* in the image of God. I now know this means we are all equally divine.

When I met you ten months ago in the Detention Center, you were quiet, just turned nineteen. You told me how you were afraid, threatened by gang violence back in El Salvador. You came to America, ended up homeless. You didn't know much about me. But every week before I left, we would pray. We would hold hands and speak to God in Spanish.

I thought you didn't like me much at first. But you received your father's number one day, your father who is an American citizen and whom you don't know. You were trying to follow perhaps the most important of the ten commandments: honor your father and mother. You asked me to call him. I called him three times before I realized it was a wrong number.

One day, you asked me to send you a Qur'an. You were curious about Islam; you had a Saudi roommate in the detention center. Blessed are you, Lord our God, who commands us to study Torah.

A month later, it was Christmas time, and we sent you a holiday card. You sent me back a beautiful card you bought in the detention center commissary. A card shaped like a house with windows you could see through, with flaps that opened to four full pages on which you wrote to me. You apologized that all you could send was ésta humilde carta. You deserve more, you wrote.

That card was your world, one of the only things you could buy in detention. You did not have a home, yet you bought me a house. I hung it up outside my bedroom door, like a *mezuzah* to remind me of my faith every time I came home. God is everywhere.

You said you were honored to be my little brother. How good and pleasant it is, to sit together as brothers and sisters.

I started telling you more about my friends, my family, my hopes and fears. Telling you things that bothered me. Like when you used the word *maricón* to refer to LGBT asylum seekers in detention. You listened intently, you asked me, it doesn't bother you if two men get married? I said not at all. We are all equal, we are all divine. You asked me what it was like to be Jewish, if I believed in Jesus. I wrote your name in Hebrew on a slip of paper; you gave me a bracelet with the Virgin of Guadalupe off your own wrist and slid it onto my right hand. If I forget you, Jerusalem, let me forget my right hand.

You lost your case. You got a lawyer; you appealed. You held faith and hope much stronger than when I first met you. You forgave your mother for not speaking to you. In that concrete-walled visitation room, you would cheer me up when I was down. You would make me laugh, ask me when I was going to buy a car, have kids, finally learn to cook like my mom.

You received your deportation papers last week. You wish to be free. I know God is everywhere, M, but the violence and injustice of gangs and extreme poverty in El Salvador mean that, right now, the brutality of humankind has won out over God in your hometown. You are divine, just like me, like all of us who won some lottery and were born with American citizenship. You deserve to pursue a good path, to look for God wherever God may be, to have parents who respect you as you respect them. To be a parent who is honored and loved, one day.

How good and pleasant it has been to sit with you, brother. Every week when we prayed, you were grateful and devout. You gave me hope, as I prayed unsteadily in Spanish and you squeezed my hand. God is everywhere. Even in a drab room in a detention center where the U.S. government pays a private corporation to imprison men and women seeking a better life.

How can God be everywhere, how can all human beings be equally divine, when you spent a year in detention, when you are now being sent back to a place where your life will be in danger? I don't know. But though you are Pentecostal and I am Jewish, you have taught me how to keep my faith and keep going in the face of unanswerable questions.

Until soon, *hermano*. *Un abrazo fuerte*,

Maya

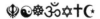

Khaled Khalili *is a student at Westminster College in Fulton, Missouri. He is majoring in Psychology and is considering a minor in Women and*

Gender Studies. He is a graphic designer who claims both Syria and Palestine as his homelands, and he spent the last of his high school years at the United World College of Costa Rica, surrounded by beautiful beaches.

We Are One Body

I am, in many ways, a person without a country. I was born and grew up in Yarmouk, the largest Palestinian refugee camp in Syria. When I was a child, more than 100,000 people called Yarmouk home, and the vast majority of those in the camp were Muslim.

Schooling in the camp included courses in Islam from the third grade until the end of our education. As a child I remember studying the Hadith of the Prophet Muhammed, including one that states "the parable of the believers in their affection, mercy, and compassion for each other is that of a body. When any limb aches, the whole body reacts with sleeplessness and fever" (Sahi Al Muslim 6586). This Hadith stuck with me well into adulthood. It tells us that we are not true Muslims unless we believe that when one human being hurts, we all hurt.

I was ten years old in 2006. Israel was attacking Lebanon. The Lebanese had to flee and, since Syria is the closest country to Lebanon from the west, many of them came to Syria. The majority of those fleeing found themselves in refugee camps, including mine.

I remember when they began arriving in the camp. At first, they didn't know where to go. The imams in our camp began to welcome the refugees into the mosques, offering our houses of worship as places of shelter and safety for those who were arriving. The mosques in the camp are just buildings used for prayer. They have running water but they don't have other resources such as food or the items a family needs to survive, and so the imams began to ask the residents of the camp for help.

First, they called for food. A short time after the call went out, my mother had just finished preparing a dish; and when we called mosques to see if they still needed food, they let us know that within ten minutes they had received enough food to feed the refugees for several weeks.

We gathered at the mosque for Friday prayers the day the Lebanese began arriving, and those leading the prayers focused on the refugees and what we, as Muslims, were called to do to help. Even though the majority of Lebanon is Christian, I do not recall anyone at the mosque even mentioning that. Instead, they spoke of the Hadith I learned in my childhood, reminding us that when anyone suffers, we all suffer, and so we must do what we can to address any human pain, whether those hurting are Muslim or not. That day we were all one. At the end of prayers the imams told us the mosques were not equipped to host people overnight, so we invited the refugees into our homes. We lived in tight quarters, but we knew as Muslims it was our task to care for those who were hurting. My Mom and Dad brought a family into our small home even though we had never met them before. We knew it was the right thing to do.

The camp is a very concentrated place, made up of tall buildings spaced very closely to each other, and the alleys are quite small. After prayer on the day the Lebanese began arriving, people from each mosque drove vans through the alleys of the camp; and as the vans passed by, residents of the camp threw items that could not be broken through the windows of their homes, and the drivers would collect them: mattresses, clothes, and all the others things these men, women, and children might need. All around the camp, everywhere I looked, Muslims were doing their best to care for Christians; Palestinian refugees were reaching out to Lebanese fleeing their homeland. It was a powerful sight.

This situation didn't last very long. As the fighting in Lebanon lessened, those fleeing the violence began to return home. Some of the Lebanese ended up staying to live in the camp, but most did not. However, this was not the only incident for which we opened our doors for those in need. When fighting in Iraq began, and recently when the Syrian revolution became a Syrian civil war, a similar series of events unfolded. Those living in the camp offered their homes, their food, and their houses of worship to those in need.

The media often portray Muslims as terrorists or violent; but when I think of Islam, I think of those who care for others, who seek to spread peace and love and do what they can to help their neighbors. It was true in my home of Yarmouk and it is true now of the majority of Muslims around the world.

♇☯✹࿊✡✝☪

Lynn Harper *began her Bodhisattva journey in the Christian Church (Disciples of Christ), where she was first inspired to bear witness on social justice issues. Since 1991, Lynn has gratefully practiced Nichiren Buddhism in connection with the Soka Gakkai International (SGI-USA) organization. Her Buddhist practice led her back to activism as an adult, focusing on eradicating oppression, dismantling the School-to-Prison Pipeline, and animal rights. Lynn holds a K-12 English as a Second Language teaching license in Minnesota and serves as a teacher-leader and trainer in Minneapolis Public Schools. When not rabble-rousing, Lynn enjoys spending time with her daughter, Libby Qi.*

Purpose and Presence

"My stepfather is a minister." That's how I explain my conversion to Buddhism as a young adult. If that doesn't make sense to you, you probably didn't spend formative years staring at the charred underbelly of religious life through an insider lens. I was deeply searching for something the *Lotus Sutra* describes as *honmak kukyo to*[2]—consistency from beginning to end. The consistency I found in the church was not as I wanted, and I became disillusioned. What I saw from my insider seat didn't match what I believed—that faith drives life: our purchases, our decisions, our participation. That we are called to serve, because much has been given us, and much is expected.

In my Buddhist practice I found a way to serve that made sense to me. Nichiren, a 13th-century Japanese priest and social reformer, taught that our fundamental identity is Buddhahood *just as we are.* Enlightenment is our birthright. We choose to be born into this life circumstance, into an injured time, in order to actualize the Bodhisattva Vow in the world according to our unique circumstances. Nichiren wrote in a letter to a practitioner,

> "All bodhisattvas take the four universal vows. And if they do not fulfill the first of those four vows, which says: 'Living beings are numberless: I vow to save them,' then they can

---

[2]From Soka Gakkai International, SGI-USA, resource, http://www.sgi-usa.org/memberresources/study/2016_essentials_part2/docs/eng/EssentialsExam2_p46_BuddhistConcepts-ThreeThousandRealmsSingleMomentLife.pdf.

hardly claim to have fulfilled the fourth vow, which says: 'Enlightenment is supreme: I vow to attain it.'"[3]

I was at home with my daughter when the events of September 11, 2001, occurred. I turned to CNN just before the second plane hit the World Trade Center. I didn't know in the moment that a Buddhist lay leader with whom I had worked closely was on that plane. "David"—a name that was easy for Americans to say— came to the United States in order to help regular people practice Buddhism. He shared his teacher's belief that the United States was a pivotal location in the spread of Buddhism from East to West. As a multicultural, multiethnic superpower in a nuclear world, the U.S. held a key position in securing peace. If the values of Buddhist humanism could spread here, the impact would change the trajectory of the entire world from war to peace. David's efforts had introduced many people to Buddhism and to the foundations of practice for self and others.

As I struggled to make sense of this tragedy, I equally struggled with the violence that erupted after. Some Americans were lashing out at a perceived enemy "other." Muslims were targeted, but not just Muslims. Anyone with a covered head or an accent was suspect. In crisis, some reverted to xenophobia and religious intolerance. While coming together around nationalistic themes, we were splintering along lines of language, culture, and ethnicity. The vision of unity and peace that David had received from his mentor, held in his heart, and devoted his life to realizing was slipping away in a chaotic aftermath.

At that point, I felt angry. Buddhism describes anger as one of ten states of being, all of which contain the potential to create value. In my moment of anger, I made a vow of faith: David's death would not become a cause for violence and hatred against fellow travelers. I vowed to somehow position myself on the frontlines of this battle in order to advocate for immigrants and reopen spaces for tolerance and healing through education. This vow aligned my work with the great lineage of teachers within my Buddhist tradition who

---

[3]"Persons of the Two Vehicles and Bodhisattvas Cannot Attain Buddha-hood in the Pre-Lotus Sutra Teachings," *The Writings of Nichiren Daishonin* (Soka Gakkai): vol. 2, p. 175, available online at https://www.nichirenlibrary. org/en/wnd-2/Content/183.

sought educational reform as a means to social reform based on Buddhist humanism. I became a teacher of English to speakers of other languages.

Since 2006, I have worked with immigrant and non-immigrant speakers of languages other than English in urban schools. Fortuitously, I am in the exact right place for this vow to unfold, because Minnesota has a tremendous history of migration and refugee resettlement. As a monolingual white woman, I am an imperfect and improbable advocate. The students and families I serve do not see themselves in me; they see a stranger. The school system recognizes me as an insider, but it often does not see the needs of the students and families I serve. Through my consistent presence, may I bring attention and action.

With humility, I remember the vow of Bodhisattva Shrimala, "If I see lonely people, people who have been jailed unjustly and have lost their freedom, people who are suffering from illness, disaster or poverty, I will not abandon them. I will bring them spiritual and material comfort."[4] I respectfully offer my support without expectation of acceptance or rejection. I understand the purpose of my presence in schools because I understand my vow. Today, again, as I develop in compassion and wisdom, may I act with courage and humility within an imperfect system.

Ϙ☯✿ॐ✡✝☾

Vy Nguyen *enjoys getting dirt under his fingernails and playing in his vegetable garden. He regularly finds himself in the kitchen after a long day with his wife and five-year-old son as they prepare and cook food together. He is involved with several non-profits in the Bay Area working to help refugees transition to the United States. After arriving in the United States from Viet Nam as a kid from a refugee camp, Vy grew up in Texas and was raised in the Christian Church (Disciples of Christ). He is currently the Executive Director for Week of Compassion, the relief, refugee, and development mission fund for the Christian Church (Disciples of Christ).*

---

[4]Daisaku Ikeda, D. "Thoughts on Education for Global Citizenship," In *A New Humanism: The University Addresses of Daisaku Ikeda* (New York: I. B. Tauris, 2010), 56.

The God of Many Tongues

Every night when I was a kid, adults would tell folk stories from our homeland of Viet Nam. We didn't have bedtime books as refugees, because we had to be ready to travel from one country to the next to find safety. So at night, the adults shared with us stories from our ancestral homeland. Only four years old, I fell asleep without fear, because our stories provided safety for me. I carry those powerful stories with me, even decades after my childhood in refugee camps.

During the 1960s, '70s, and '80s, Southeast Asia was full of conflict and wars. Millions fled their home countries in hope of finding a new place to live, including me. Every night, as part of my bedtime ritual, I asked the adults, "Where will we go next?" They didn't know the answer, but what were they supposed to tell a scared four-year-old? I remember that they dreamed about the new homeland with me. They dreamed about children being able to play on the playground without worry for their safety. They dreamed about things as foreign as snow! Above all, the adults dreamed that the children would one day be able to go to sleep at night, safe, without nightmares. I am sure the adults knew how the stuff of nightmares could so easily become reality after so many years of war and turmoil. We all hoped that soon, safety and possibility would be more than just a dream.

Today, when I hear about the global refugee crisis, I think of not only my own experience, but of the experiences of the millions of refugees from the past through today. As children, we didn't think much of the risks our parents took, nor did we think fully about how they left everything behind to find a new life where we would be safe.

There was safety on the other side, and my faith is centered in that experience and in a community in the United States, a church community specifically, who welcomed me and helped to transform a foreign land into my new home. Through the breaking of bread and sharing of many meals, all sacred, the United States became my home. The church offered me a community of acceptance and compassion, one where I was no longer a scared stranger.

Since my childhood, the parable of the good Samaritan has resonated with me. It is a story of strangers encountering one another, even though it was full of risk. The parable tells of a Jewish man on the road to Jericho who was beaten and robbed, but no one stopped to help him. The priest and the Levite did not stop because the road was too dangerous and they didn't want to risk their lives for his. But then came a Samaritan, who, upon seeing the injured man, stopped and offered his help. It didn't matter that the injured man was Jewish, even though there were tensions between Jews and Samaritans. It did not matter to the Samaritan, who felt compassion for the injured man and risked his own life on this dangerous road.

The scripture reminds me that God shows up in unexpected and, sometimes, unsafe places. God shows up and is vulnerable with the vulnerable (Christ's incarnation is the most spectacular example of exactly this!). As followers of God, Christians are called to do the same. Sometimes it involves taking a risk like that good Samaritan. When we do, we encounter God. In the weak and vulnerable stranger we experience our Creator. Because all are created in God's image, we are made siblings.

At this particular moment there are more than 65 million displaced persons and refugees worldwide. This is the highest number we have seen in recorded history. It seems daunting. How can we be the Samaritan to millions of people in need?

To answer that question, let me tell you about the Christian church to which I belong:

We are still the church that welcomed a small and frightened boy from Viet Nam over three decades ago. We are still the church that answers God's call to put everything aside—our fear, our uncertainty, our safety—for those who seek refuge. We are still the church that listens to the stories of our siblings, of their faith, and that sees the image of God in many faces and hears the words of God in many tongues. We encounter our humanity by bridging divides and allowing God to claim us all as God's children.

We are called to take that risk and welcome the millions of children who are trying to go to bed without fear each night. It is my prayer that we be the refuge from nightmares and the bearers of good dreams.

Kelly Cohen-Mazurowski *works as Director of Academic Engagement at Duke University, where she advises students on opportunities for global and civic engagement. In her spare time, she volunteers with refugees in Durham, North Carolina. She has a Master of Divinity degree from Duke University and a B.A. degree from Wheaton College.*

Extending Welcome

My father's side of the family came to the United States around 1900. My great-great-grandfather Kalmos Rubenstein was a Jewish man from Suwalki, on the far eastern edge of Poland. He and his brothers left because they feared conscription into the army. I imagine that they would have preferred to stay at home. They knew the language. They knew the customs. They knew how to make lives for themselves in Poland. Instead, they faced the challenge of starting new lives in the United States.

On census documents from the turn of the century, Kalmos's job is listed as "junk seller." He didn't strike it rich in Cleveland, Ohio. He didn't live the American Dream, complete with a house surrounded by a white picket fence. But he did find a place where he could live without fear of persecution for his faith or his political beliefs.

I am thankful for the legacy his story leaves me. In my volunteer work with refugees, I often reflect not only on Kalmos's journey but also on the community that received him. Because someone welcomed Kalmos, because someone taught him how to speak English, because someone helped him learn to navigate a new city, I am here today.

Like me, many people feel that we should welcome strangers because our own families were welcomed in this country. For Christians and Jews, the call to welcome the stranger extends beyond our own family histories. The book of Leviticus says, "The alien who resides with you shall be to you as the citizen among you; you shall love the alien as yourself, for you were aliens in the land of Egypt: I am the Lord your God" (Leviticus 19:34). Our common history is a history of aliens and strangers. Our story is an immigrant story, and whenever we encounter the immigrant, we encounter one who shares our story. In this way the author of Leviticus enjoins all of us to remember that there is no us and them. There is only us.

Today, refugees join us from different parts of the world than my ancestors did. Instead of Ireland, Italy, and Poland, they come from Somalia, Iraq, and Syria. Though they speak different languages and practice different religions than my ancestors, they share the same hope that they will be welcomed here. Mere admittance into our country is not the same as being welcomed. When refugees arrive, they come with skills, intelligence, and a desire to succeed, but they need help learning how to navigate life in a new country. This might mean assistance with filling out a job application, learning how to shop at an American grocery store, or reading a bus schedule. These are simple things that anybody can assist with, and they help refugees thrive in their new neighborhoods. Yet when you begin to give this simple kind of help, you realize you aren't the only one doing welcoming work.

The other day I was visiting a refugee family from the Democratic Republic of Congo. They arrived in the U.S. about two years ago. In addition to working as dishwashers and housekeepers, the family has a business braiding hair. Often when I come to visit, strangers from Ghana, Nigeria, and Central African Republic are sitting on the floor having their hair plaited. Last week when I came to visit for conversation practice, one of the daughters quietly pulled my hair down from its ponytail and divided it into sections. Without saying anything, she wove my hair into circuitous braids. I'm not sure if she did it because I looked like a mess (I probably did) or because of our friendship, but this simple act showed me that she was comfortable enough to come close. Though she's Muslim and I'm Christian, though she's black and I'm white, though her first language is Lingala and mine is English, she welcomed me.

We remember that most of our ancestors came from other countries. We remember God's command to love the alien as ourselves. We remember that we are more alike than we are different. And we find that as we welcome, that welcome is returned.

Reflection Questions

- Kelly Cohen-Mazurowski writes about her ancestor who immigrated to the United States. Do you know what country/countries your ancestors originated from and how your family ended up where it lives today? How does your family's story shape your views on immigration?

- Vy Nguyen points out that the current refugee crisis in our world can feel overwhelming. What resources does your faith offer you in the face of overwhelming problems and unanswerable questions? How do you think your faith community is called to begin addressing the current refugee and immigration situation?

- Khaled Khalili writes about welcoming Lebanese refugees into their already crowded refugee camp in Syria and generously sharing food and necessities. What in your religious teachings promotes an attitude of abundance that encourages sharing what you have? How do attitudes about the scarcity or abundance of resources influence our attitudes about welcoming refugees and immigrants?

- Maya Wahrman's Jewish tradition taught her that God is everywhere and that all humans are created in God's image. How can people who are very different from you help you to experience the divine or to see God more clearly?

- Maya Wahrman expresses gratitude for the relationship of mutual care and concern that develops between herself and the young man in detention she visited. What is the difference between helping someone less privileged than you and working for justice alongside people facing oppression?

- Lynn Harper shares the Buddhist teaching that any state of being, including anger, has the potential to create value. What situations in today's world make you angry? How could you channel that anger into meaningful action?

Sexuality and Gender Identity

Jamie Lynn's Introduction

There are places in our lives where religion often helps, and there are places where religion can hurt. Sexuality, historically, has been an aspect of the human experience where religion has done damage. Throughout history religion has attempted to place boundaries around sex and the human sexual experience. Whether out of fear or the desire to control, people of faith have often subscribed to ideas about "right" and "wrong" concepts of sexuality, relationships, and sexual practices. These clear definitions of "right" and "wrong" have left many feeling isolated and alienated from faith and religion. When you are told that who you love or how you identify is sinful or broken, you are given the message that the divine does not claim you, that you are somehow flawed and unworthy of love.

As a queer woman in ministry, I am often invited to speak about the intersection of sexuality and Christianity. I once preached at a summer pride celebration in Springfield, Missouri. It was a joyful day; there were rainbows and symbols of love and acceptance everywhere. It was a true representation of what it looks like when we allow ourselves to love and to fully embrace the diversity and entirety of the human community. Several faith communities had booths and proclaimed, with their presence and their signs, that

God does indeed love everyone. One church, National Avenue
Christian Church (Disciples of Christ) passed out homemade loaves
of bread to share their belief that *all* are welcome at God's table.

There were also some Christian congregations who protested the
pride celebration. They placed three massive wooden crosses at the
edge of the gathering and held signs with disparaging, sometimes
violent, remarks about the LGBTQIA+ community. When those
celebrating pride walked by, they condemned them to hell and
called them names. For many who identify as lesbian, gay, bisexual,
transgender, queer, intersex, asexual, or otherwise, this was not
surprising. Often, their primary association and experience with
religion is hate.

Hate is not the prevailing message taught by most sacred texts.
They call us to love and love well, and in doing so we witness to
the love of the divine. Verses in 1 John 4 within the Christian New
Testament read, "Beloved, let us love one another, because love is
from God; everyone who loves is born of God and knows God.
Whoever does not love does not know God, for God is love" (1
John 4:7–8). In the Hebrew Bible, Genesis reminds us that we are
made in the image of God. Gay or straight, intersex or transgender,
all of us carry the divine spark, and we are worthy of great love.

The stories in this chapter explore what it means, from a variety
of faith traditions, to rejoice and celebrate the multitude of ways
humans express their sexuality and sexual identities. It is my
great hope that with enough conversation, enough shared stories,
enough commitment to truly loving one another, religion will
become a source of help rather than harm, of love rather than hate.

☸☪✡☽☆✝☪

Miri Mogilevsky *is a first-generation immigrant from a secular Russian
Jewish family. Born in Haifa, Israel, to parents who had recently fled the
Soviet Union, she is now settled happily in Columbus, Ohio, with two
cats and many, many plants. A graduate of Northwestern University
and Columbia University School of Social Work, Miri is a clinical social
worker who practices therapy with LGBTQ and HIV-positive clients.
She also teaches seventh-grade Sunday School at Congregation Tifereth
Israel and writes an advice column called "Yours in Tenacity" for fellow*

breast cancer survivors at Healthline.com. She enjoys reading, writing, gardening, rock climbing, hiking, cooking, and biking.

Repairing the World

Long before the modern gay rights movement—before same-sex marriage, before Ellen DeGeneres, before Stonewall—a Jewish woman bravely came out of the closet, risking her life to do so.

She had kept her identity secret because of hatred and stigma. Like many others, she lived a double life to keep herself safe. But silence wasn't an option forever. If things were to ever get better for people like her, she would have to speak out. Using her privilege and her words, she did.

No, she wasn't a lesbian—at least not as far as we know. She was Queen Esther, who "came out" as a Jew to her husband, King Ahasuerus of Persia, saving the Jewish people from genocide. Every year, Jewish people around the world celebrate her bravery during the holiday of Purim.

I don't believe that everything in the Bible really happened as described. But the power of these stories isn't in whether they're literally true or not—it's in what they teach us and how they make us feel. The story of Esther makes me feel a lot of things: pride, because I share a heritage with someone who demonstrated such bravery and selflessness. Joy, because that particular story ended so happily. Sadness, for everyone who suffered before Esther was able to put an end to it. Anger, because of the risk she had to take, because she was the one who had to fix the problem even though she hadn't created it.

As a queer woman, I think about this story a lot when I despair of how broken our world is, and how those of us who take responsibility for fixing it are almost never the ones who broke it. The Jewish concept of *tikkun olam*—repairing the world—guides us to leave this place better than we found it regardless of who's to blame. And, of course, we're all at least a little bit to blame.

Stories like this one remind me why I believe that Judaism compels us to stand with all marginalized people. Just as there are parallels between Esther's coming out story and my own, there are parallels between the oppression of Jewish people and all other oppressions. The Torah itself makes this comparison: "You too must befriend the stranger, for you were strangers in the land of Egypt." (Deuteronomy 10:19, Sefaria). Countless rabbis, leaders, and ordinary Jews like me have agreed with this over the centuries and have tried to live their lives by it. This tradition is part of the reason I feel comfortable being out as queer in almost any Jewish space except for the most traditional synagogues and communities.

That's not to say it's always easy. I find myself alienated by the emphasis on marrying and having babies, the gender-essentialist assumptions about who's "naturally suited" to what, the fact that most synagogue leaders are still straight, cisgender men. It's easy to find abhorrently homophobic content in the Torah and in the writings of the rabbis. Yet it's also easy to find synagogues with floats in the Pride parade, straight cisgender Jewish people speaking out in support of LGBTQ rights, and Jewish texts spanning the centuries that show a remarkably flexible understanding of gender and sexuality. In the early 14th century, a French-Jewish scholar named Kalonymus ben Kalonymus wrote a gut-wrenching poem[1] about wishing God had made him a woman. Today, Kalonymus would find herself welcomed at my synagogue.

There are plenty of Jewish people who attest that Judaism is clear on the issue of sexuality: sex is to take place between a man and a woman, and only within the boundaries of marriage; and your gender is what the doctor calls out when you're born. Plenty of Jewish people find same-sex relationships morally wrong and disgusting. Unfortunately (or fortunately, depending on your point of view), the rest of us don't get to disown these Jews and claim that they just didn't read the texts or listen to their rabbi carefully enough. That's not how Judaism works. You read the texts and listen to the rabbis, and then you use your head and form your own opinion.

Some might read the story of Esther and see nothing other than a lesson on the value of bravery and protecting your own. I see a resounding call to speak up, to value and protect not just our own but the differences between us. That call echoes down the centuries. I hear it in the deeds of Jewish people who have fought for social justice throughout history. I hear it in the words of Jewish people

---

[1] "Even Bohen," found at https://www.sefaria.org/sheets/135628?lang=bi.

who speak up for our Muslim neighbors and would-be neighbors. I hear it in my own work. I hear it every day as I try, however imperfectly, to help repair the world and make it whole.

☬☸❀ॐ☯✝☪

Pastor Marquis Hairston is the founder and Senior Pastor of The City Church of Charlotte, North Carolina, and is currently pursuing a Master of Divinity at Wake Forest University. As an African American, same-gender–loving, Pentecostal faith leader and social advocate, he is passionate about being a voice crying out on behalf of underrepresented populations. He is a father to one son, and he endeavors to do his part to create a world where his son will not have to endure some of the societal struggles of our current time.

Unapologetically Pentecostal

I am a Pentecostal. I am an African American Pentecostal. I am an openly gay and affirming Pentecostal. I can identify candidly as both black and gay *because* I am Pentecostal. Allow me to explain.

I was raised by my paternal grandparents. From the age of six, I felt that I was different from almost everyone I met. My family gave me the language to articulate this feeling as the "Call of God on my life"—more specifically, a call to preach the gospel. I picked up very early that this Call on my life was a good thing, one that I should pursue wholeheartedly.

My first service as a pastor was when I refurbished an old wooden picnic table into a pulpit, tied a towel around my neck, grabbed my children's Bible, and went outside to "play church" in my grandparents' backyard with neighborhood friends. We would sing and shout, and I would preach and lay hands on the children until we all gyrated and whirled around to the movement of the Spirit.

One day, something took hold of me, and I began to cry out in a voice that was so passionate my grandfather came rushing out of the house and angrily tried to stop me from disturbing the rest of the neighborhood. I began to cry and shout even more, with tears running down my face. I began to say that God was real and that God was going to raise me up to preach the gospel. I was totally consumed by the Spirit, and I spoke in an unknown tongue, as the Holy Spirit gave me utterance. I was six years old.

I was licensed to preach at age 17. Struggling to reconcile my sexuality and my spirituality, I married a woman, and from our union a son was born. Shortly after our marriage ended, I realized that my sexuality was something I could not ignore.

I credit my Pentecostal roots for my coming out process. As Pentecostals, we believe that one day, God poured out God's Spirit upon flesh. This resulted in thousands of people being added to God's church on Pentecost. This day was trademarked by the supernatural ability of people to "talk in tongues." Upon deeper reflection, I learned that something else happened that day. The ending verses of Acts 2 say that after the people finished talking in tongues, they all gave their possessions to the church so that the leadership could redistribute the resources, so that everyone had all things in common. That's social justice!

The pouring out of God's Spirit on Pentecost prompted a movement toward social justice, not just eternal salvation and security. Today, as an openly gay Pentecostal pastor, I believe that the work of the church is to do just as they did on that day: to be prophetic witnesses against the injustices of our present time. Pentecost wasn't just about getting the Spirit into humankind, it was about connecting humankind with itself, so that through the Spirit and love, we can find unity without uniformity.

I lost everything to come out. My wife and I never had the chance to celebrate the birth of our son or our first wedding anniversary; I did not have the chance to be in my son's life without interference from family, courts, and the Department of Social Services; I was excommunicated from the church family I loved deeply and served earnestly; other churches and ministries ended their fellowship with me, because I was the newly exposed gay preacher who could not keep his own family together. I suffered financially after a broken lease, child support, and job loss due to lack of transportation. I even had to drop out of college.

Even with all the losses, I have gained more than I could imagine by living my authentic truth. Although it took time, I have begun to see recovery and restoration happen in every area of my life. My son and I have an awesome relationship; I founded the affirming and inclusive ministry we affectionately call "The City Church," which is thriving in Charlotte, North Carolina; and hundreds, if not thousands, have been positively impacted by my personal testimony concerning my journey. I have also founded a faith-based non-profit organization called the "City Nation" to educate, empower, and eradicate HIV/AIDS and anything that furthers the marginalization, exclusion, or oppression of people because of who they are.

The scriptures admonish us to worship God in Spirit and in truth. People may not understand our truth, but our job is to be loving and to make Christ known in the earth through and by the love we have for the "other." The City Church is founded on such a principle: We exist to Love God (in all of God's manifestations). Love (all) People. Everywhere. Everyday! I would not have such a rich framework for a social justice ministry without my experience as a Pentecostal. I am unapologetically Pentecostal, and I will always seek to make Christ accessible to "the least of these."

☬☉✻ॐ✡✡†☾

Ameera Khan *is a DevOps Engineer at Mobile Doorman in Madison, Wisconsin. She graduated from St. Louis University with a Bachelor's of Science in BioElectronics Engineering and minors in Math and Computer Science. She interned with the Council of American-Islamic Relations, created spiritual space for queer and trans people with Metro Trans Umbrella Group and the El-Tawhid Juma Circle – Madison, and was president of the Interfaith Alliance at SLU. She is a member of Advocates for Youth's Muslim Youth Leadership Council, which aims to create resources for queer and trans Muslim youth and advocate for their sexual and reproductive rights while maintaining a strong connection to Islam spiritually and culturally.*

A Good Muslim

I was brought up by Bengali immigrant parents near St. Louis, Missouri, with values of hard work and strict religion. These happen to be typical Midwestern conservative values, except my religion was Islam instead of Evangelical Christianity. I was expected to "be a good Muslim" from a young age, and I tried my damnedest to be that good Muslim and make my parents proud. My mother's strict interpretation of Islam taught that good Muslims do not listen to music, so I stuffed my fingers in my ears during first-grade music class while praying five times a day.

There were many other Bengalis, as well as Indians, Pakistanis, and Arabs, in the St. Louis Muslim community, the vast majority from immigrant families. Although the Muslim community was diverse, almost everyone I interacted with was financially better off than my family. While I looked at other kids with their flashy Game Boy Advances, I was taught to be frugal with the little I had. My mom taught me to value myself not based on the worth of my bank accounts but on the worth of my faith. In fifth grade, I became a member of the first generation of Huffaz in the St. Louis area. Huffaz are people who have memorized the entire Qur'an in Arabic. It was two years of rigorous work, but the support I felt from my family and community spurred me on, as well as internal motivation to grow in my faith and be a good Muslim.

I entered high school and slowly realized I was gay. This took a huge toll on me emotionally and spiritually, and much of high school was plagued with my wrestling with God. Nobody knew I was gay. If they did, I knew what they would tell me: that I had a mental defect, and the only way I could truly live as a Muslim while being gay would be to never have sex, never find love and be loved, never be married—to force myself into living hell so I could find heaven after death. This hopelessness dragged me through years of depression and suicidal ideation. I finally found one valuable friend who helped me accept that God had a reason for creating me the way I am, and that my "test" is not to live stifled by shallow interpretations of a book with thousands of years of context haphazardly interpolated. Rather, my test is to be humble and genuine, accepting and understanding, even in the face of those who will humiliate me and not afford me respect.

My first two years of college were similar to high school, as I still lived with my parents. Near the end of sophomore year I grew close with an upperclassman who happened to be gay, and he helped me become more confident. I came out of the closet to my close friends, and on a stage at a spoken word event with five hundred Muslims in attendance. It was exhilarating to finally begin living as myself. But my parents, with whom I still lived, became emotionally abusive, as they could not accept me as I needed to be. Fortunately, I was offered a position as a Resident Assistant in a dorm, was able to move onto campus, and found an acceptance that was completely foreign to my strict upbringing. It was the breath of fresh air I desperately needed.

I began pushing myself outside of my comfort zone, and my eyes opened to systems of injustice. I traveled to the U.S.-Mexico border and saw firsthand how deeply justice work and faith must be intertwined. The idea of intersectionality, of all struggles for justice being part of the same movement for liberation, was new to me, but it made so much sense. I realized my own identity was intersectional, as a gay Muslim child of immigrants. Before, I had only known about the marginalization of the Muslim community in America. Now, I learned about the systematic marginalization of the African-American community, the struggles of the LGBT community, and how the undercurrents of history continue today. I joined Black Lives Matter activists in their protests against police brutality. I realized I carried the scars of unaddressed traumas due to these systems that failed so many people like me. I realized I wasn't a gay male, but a genderfluid trans woman.

These social justice issues made me see my role as a Muslim—a believer in a just, merciful, and loving Allah—in a completely new light. My purpose in life, my role as a good Muslim, is to stand for the oppressed. I began speaking with my legislators and advocating on issues such as the Dream Act and the modern-day Rohingya Genocide. I continue trying to accompany and empower those who remain marginalized.

☬☸✡ॐ☥✝☪

Andrew Huffman *is a nonbinary witch college student at Warren Wilson College in Swannanoa, North Carolina. They are active in interfaith work due to a passion to ease this tumultuous time by bringing together faiths in our world. They seek to educate through stories, both nonfiction and fiction.*

The Tiger and the Sparrow

My faith was solidified the day I started taking testosterone. I had been struggling to survive in the wrong body. I'm a transgender teenager, and no one would take me seriously when I tried to explain that my gender dysphoria[2] was destroying my mental health. That day, I thanked the universe for giving me the chance to start the hormone that would change my life. I thanked whomever was listening for protecting me the day before, and I lit a candle to allow me to pray to the crystals and statues on my altar for giving me power throughout the night. I then blew out the candle, put on the necklace I was drawn to that morning, and went to start my day. Because I was going to meet new people, I prayed that I would not make a fool of myself, offend anyone, be misgendered, and that my mannerisms would be as masculine as possible. These were little utterances under my breath that gave me the strength to get through a day that would make or break my mental health.

Witchcraft, the faith tradition I practice, is as individual as the people who practice it. One method I practice is divination. I find some of my instruction from tarot, a way of divination that uses designated cards. So when I encounter a moral dilemma, I do a tarot reading, and the energy of the universe will tell me what to do. In fact, I usually know what the answer is before the reading: accept others and yourself. Another way I practice my faith is using crystals to help amplify energy around me, whether it's in a necklace or a stone that I gift to my friend to help her through a rough day. I also create spells to chant, draw powerful symbols called sigils, and make jars filled with herbs that correspond to different meanings.

When it feels as if North Carolina, where I go to college, and the United States as a whole are pushing back against me, I light some candles and incense, cling to my black tourmaline, and pray. Black tourmaline is a strong crystal that shields me from external and internal negative energy. Prayer will not change others' minds, but it will change mine. It will turn my defeated energy into a fire that

---

[2]Gender dysphoria, as defined by the American Psychiatric Association, "involves a conflict between a person's physical or assigned gender and the gender with which he/she/they identify." More information can be found here: https://www.psychiatry.org/patients-families/gender-dysphoria/what-is-gender-dysphoria.

will protect myself and others. I need that fire especially when I am told that my gender identity is not valid and that I am not allowed to use the restroom associated with my identity.

When I face that, I tell myself over and over that the world has made both the tiger and the sparrow, two animals that are complete opposites but live on this planet together. It may seem insignificant to some, but to me it shows that the universe has made us all in different forms because we are meant to be here. We are all a gift that the universe has given itself, and I choose to love every gift from the universe.

There are even some practicing witches who say transgender and queer people are not welcome in the tradition. Their belief is that only cisgender, straight women should practice witchcraft. I have been personally attacked for appropriating a faith tradition that originally had no strict guidelines. That is hard for me to stomach, because I see witchcraft as something that we nurture and that nurtures us. Why would this way of life restrict who prays? I understand that I have a rather broad, community-oriented understanding, but it's still hard.

In response to pushback, I first and foremost refuse to give up my practice. I pray that the universe will aid me in my life, and I feel that support every day. When I stop feeling called to that path, I will move on. But no resistance will pull me from my calling: to help others who feel as trapped as I did. I can help others who feel like they will never be accepted—the drag queen, the closeted nonbinary kid, the lesbian couple down the street, and the asexual stuck in a sexual relationship they don't want—by showing them that they are not alone and there is a light at the end of the tunnel. I was put in the world to love, not to hate. To me, hatred is merely the absence of love in a life that craves acceptance.

If I can love a homophobic or transphobic person, witch or otherwise, maybe one day they will give me my love back, and then that love can extend to other communities. Maybe not immediately, but I will pray every day that they have the most love in their life, so that one day they can.

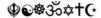

Lynn Cooper *is the Catholic Chaplain at Tufts University. She earned an M.Div. from Harvard Divinity School and is currently working on a Doctor of Ministry in Transformational Leadership at Boston University. Lynn met her partner Andrew in the storytelling scene of Boston. In this community, she fell in love with the transformation of public space into honest-to-goodness sanctuary. Watching audiences hold stories as the sacred, living things that they are has helped her to rethink how we do church. She and Andrew (a Unitarian Universalist minister and chaplain) live in a little green house in Providence, Rhode Island, with their son.*

Why Are You Here?

I sat across from Sister Margaret in her warm and welcoming office. "I know why I'm here," she said. "I joined an order 40 years ago on the other side of the world. But why are you here? Why are you in this church?" Her question rocked me. Ten years later, I continue to return to this question, and it continues to serve as my vocational compass.

As a woman and a queer person, it had been far from clear whether there was a place for me in the church of my childhood and family. I spent three years in divinity school exploring how different communities worshipped and practiced their faith, and I emerged with a wholly renewed sense of purpose and call. I had a right to be "here" and I knew it in my bones. But Sister Margaret's question brought me face-to-face with something more foundational. What can I offer this church that no one else on earth can offer? What are my unique gifts, and how will I use them to spread the gospel?

I ran into Sister Margaret three years later at the Celebration of Mary Magdalene hosted by Boston College's School of Theology and Ministry. This annual gathering attracts many sisters from around New England. I knew it was a big event, but I was not prepared for the sea of rose-printed blouses crossing Commonwealth Avenue, flooding into St. Ignatius Church. While there were men in the congregation that day, they were grossly outnumbered by women, old and young, celebrating our beloved saint.

There are some moments that change how we see the world and how our imaginations process possibility. This was one of those moments for me.

I sat in the back of the sanctuary. From there I could take in the sight before me. It was stunning, in beauty and in breadth. On the shoulders of these women was a veritable rainbow of roses—and the shoulders themselves were different shapes, some big and round and others slender and boney. Throughout the liturgy, I watched sisters smile, putting their arms around one another, greeting old friends with delight and laughter.

Every mass is a celebration, every Sunday a Little Easter, but you might not know it depending on where you worship. On that sunny July day, the sisters were so full of light, joy, and exuberance. The vitality of the roses filled the ether of St. Ignatius Church. It was contagious and nourishing. It was authentic and unselfconscious. The spirit of that day changed the way I embraced my ministry at Tufts University. If I could help folks experience even a taste of this kind of hospitality and joy, I would be doing God's work.

That fall, a first-year student asked to meet over tea. When I arrived at the café, she was already waiting for me. She was visibly nervous. We chatted a few minutes, getting to know each other a bit before she launched into her prepared words.

"I just got to Tufts and I want to be part of the LGBT community. But I also want to be part of the Catholic community. Would there be a place for me there?"

These words broke me open. On the one hand, I must have done something right if she was asking at all. But on the other, why is the bar so low? Why is this even a question? Why does this child of God, any child of God, have to bear the burden of wondering whether they are worthy of belonging? When we know that 30 to 40 percent of LGBT youth attempt suicide—a rate 1.5 to 3 times more than heterosexual youth—we must do church differently. The stakes do not get higher than human life, and that is exactly what is at stake when we do not welcome with open arms all of God's children as they are, celebrating their gifts and learning their wisdom.

This young woman brought so much to our community, but her greatest gift was living an open, authentic, and generous life as a queer Christian. Her presence testified to the truth of God's love and grace. In September, she will be starting seminary. I shudder to think that the church may have lost her and her gifts. I shudder to think of a reality wherein we missed the transformative experience of this woman distributing communion in bow tie and faux hawk.

I have the great privilege of witnessing to the beauty of the roses each Sunday as our students reach across the aisle to hold hands. At Goddard Chapel, we sing the Lord's Prayer to a most jaunty melody. The music and the roses remind me that there is joy and fullness in each of our bodies—that we are holy as we are and that God delights in our delight of one another.

Reflection Questions

- Linden Huffman points out that every creature has particular gifts it offers the universe. What unique gifts do you offer your religious community that no one else can offer? What gifts can people of diverse sexual orientations and gender identities offer your religious community?

- Who, if anyone, is excluded from full participation in the rituals, sacraments, and rites of your religious tradition? On what basis are these persons excluded? What is your view of these restrictions?

- How do you (or can you) help people from the LGBTQI+ community feel welcome and safe in your place of worship? How is offering this kind of hospitality "doing God's work," as Lynn Cooper says?

- Miri Mogilevsky draws strength as a queer woman from the courage of Queen Esther. What stories or texts in your religious tradition inspire you to speak up in the face of injustice? What texts have shaped your understanding of how LGBTQI+ people are to be treated?

- Like Ameera Khan, have you had an experience of wrestling with God, or a time in which your commitment to your religion was tested? What helped you to get through it? How did this experience impact your faith?

• Marquis Hairston has struggled to find full acceptance in the church as both a Pentecostal pastor and a gay man. When or with whom have you felt completely accepted for who you are? What were the conditions that allowed you to feel this sense of acceptance?

Gender and Women's Leadership

Jamie Lynn's Introduction

"Traveling while clergy" can be risky business. When a pastor boards a flight and buckles into the tiny airline seat, there's no telling who might sit in the adjacent seat. People bring everything with them when they board the plane, not just their luggage. They also carry their fears about religion; their own theological beliefs; their worries about judgement from pastors; their past hurts from the church; and, often, a lot of strong convictions.

As a newly ordained minister in my mid-twenties, I once took a five-hour red-eye flight from Seattle to Boston. The man next to me made polite conversation, and before the plane even took off, he asked what I did for a living. "I'm a minister," I said. He quickly responded "in a church? You're a pastor?" I nodded, and the next five hours began to unfold in ways I didn't see coming. He quickly pulled out his Bible and said with complete certainty, "Women cannot be pastors." He began with 1 Timothy 2:12: "I permit no woman to teach or to have authority over a man; she is to keep silent." In that moment, I knew it was going to be a very long flight.

Women have struggled to find their place within our religious traditions for thousands of years. Thankfully, there are holy texts and theological tenets that support them in this work. In both

Jewish and Christian scriptures, the prophet Deborah commands an army and is called by God to lead her people (Judges 4 and 5). In the Christian New Testament, Paul writes, "As many of you as were baptized into Christ have clothed yourselves with Christ. There is no longer Jew or Greek, there is no longer slave or free, there is no longer male and female; for all of you are one in Christ Jesus."

Other religious traditions engage these questions as well. What roles do women have the right to hold? Can they be leaders? Can they teach and guide God's people? The Buddha invited women into his earliest monastic community, and they were full participants. The Promulgation of Universal Peace, a core document within the Baha'i tradition, reads, "And let it be known once more that until woman and man recognize and realize equality, social and political progress here or anywhere will not be possible."[1] The Qur'an reminds us, "To whoever, male or female, does good deeds and has faith, We shall give a good life and reward them according to the best of their actions." (16:97, Abdel Haleem)

In recent news, stories from the #Metoo movement have reminded us that women continue to struggle to be seen and heard, to be valued as human beings worthy of respect in all times and in all places. The voices and experiences of women offer a powerful testimony from which all people can learn and grow in understanding. Without women's religious leadership, an essential part of the story is missing.

☬☸✡ॐ☯✝☪

Michelle Hicks *believes in the power of education to right many of the world's problems. She works with youth as an English teacher, coach, and mentor. Originally from Louisiana, she considers herself a North Carolina native but has lived as far away as Boston, California, and Ireland. Writing is one of her passions. She has published a slew of poems, ghostwrites essays of all kinds, and has a couple of novels waiting for that final revision. After becoming interested in Buddhism as a teenager, Michelle found her spiritual home in the teachings of the Buddha and the Won Buddhist community in Raleigh, North Carolina.*

---

[1] From "Talk to Federation of Women's Clubs" at Hotel LaSalle in Chicago, May 2, 1912, available at http://reference.bahai.org/en/t/ab/PUP/pup-32.html.

Her interests include running, swimming, dancing ballet, and learning to bake French pastries like a pro.

You Are Enough

There is a fundamental difference between a young woman of eleven or twelve and a young woman of fifteen or sixteen. I observe this distinction daily in my unique role teaching both sixth- and ninth-grade students. I am not talking about enthusiastic and engaged pre-teen girls becoming sullen and image-obsessed teens, although that may be true elsewhere. My ninth-graders are as active, community-minded, and intellectually curious as their younger counterparts. Rather, a young woman of twelve believes in girl power, if not outright female superiority. She knows she can do anything and is not afraid. A young woman of sixteen knows she can do anything, but she also understands that her gender may be an extra hurdle on the way to success. She's not sure what the future holds for her.

How could a few short years of life bring about such a marked change in our girls? Perhaps it correlates with the rise of media consumption in the teenage years. Perhaps the way society conditions self-doubt in female children manifests as school, athletics, and social life become more competitive and complex. I don't have the answer to that question.

These wonderful young women are plagued with worry about being "too ugly," "too emotional," "not smart enough," and just "not enough." Middle school girls and teenage boys suffer insecurities as well, but not at the rate I observe in women in their mid to late teenage years. They feel that no one trusts them, no one believes in them, and no one will protect them.

As a woman of thirty, I am still working on overcoming my own fear. I am just as quick to express doubt and self-judgement as my high school students. As a teacher, I do my best to ferry young women to the stage in their lives when they discover they can trust, believe in, and protect themselves. Fortunately, my faith provides some guidance on how to accomplish the task of combatting "not enough."

In Buddhism, women were welcomed into full participation in religious life early on. Though the Buddha at first questioned the capacity of women to join his order, he quickly welcomed nuns, *bikkihuni,* who showed commitment to achieving enlightenment. The Buddha also famously admonished a king who was upset when his wife gave birth to a baby girl. "A female child," the Buddha said, "may prove/Even a better offspring than a male/For she may grow up wise and virtuous" (Kindred Sayings 1:111). In the sixth century B.C.E., this was a remarkably progressive idea: a child's sex doesn't determine his or her worth.

However, my favorite passage about women in Buddhist scripture is not spoken by the Buddha, but by a nun. In the Sutta Pitaka, a *bikkihuni* comments simply: "What matters being a woman/if with mind firmly set/one grows in the knowledge/of the Right Law, with insight?" To me, this is a definition of true equality. Equality is not giving women a "special" place within the religious order. It is not upholding separate "feminine" virtues or spheres of influence. Equality is looking into the true nature of a person and seeing all that is good. Gender does not matter. In Buddha-speak, one might say that gender is *empty.* It is an illusion of this world with no fixed entity or permanence. We all are one in our true nature.

Of course, the reality of women practitioners of Buddhism fell short of this goal of complete equality. *Bikkihunis* were subject to restrictions that monks were not. I also don't think that it's always useful to regard sex and gender as empty—they are, after all, crucial parts of our experience of this world. Nevertheless, the teachings of Buddhism guide me in ways to support my female students. We must believe that all women are strong, capable, intelligent, and worthy. We should welcome the true, perfect nature of every woman, just as the Buddha welcomed her sisters two and a half millennia ago.

In regards to helping young women flourish when they doubt themselves, I can provide a few simple pieces of advice. Love them for themselves and not for their accomplishments. Ban the phrases "smart for a girl," "strong for a girl," or anything "for a girl," from your speech and thoughts. Let young women know that if a door is not open to them, they can open it for themselves. When they face challenges, help them dwell in the peace of their own wisdom and strength. Finally, if you are a woman, do all of this also for yourself. You are wise. You are virtuous. You are enough.

ॐ☬✡ॐ☯✝☪

Zainab Baloch has run for City Council and Mayor of Raleigh, North Carolina. She is the founder of YAP!, which provides local avenues for young people to bear witness to policy decisions and pursue accountability through voting and outspoken, unapologetic action through technology. She works for Even, a startup whose mission to end the paycheck-to-paycheck cycle goes hand in hand with her work engaging millennials in the Poor People's Campaign. She wants to empower others, especially young people, people of color, and women, to not be afraid of disrupting the system to bring about positive change.

Empowered

I chose to run for Raleigh City Council in 2017, at age twenty-six. As a first-generation American and the first-born of 6 children, I grew up learning the value of community, hard work, and resilience. My parents met in North Carolina after immigrating from Pakistan 35 years ago, and chose Raleigh as their home. Even though my parents struggled to learn a new culture, they worked hard to ensure we had the opportunities they did not. Not only did they instill the importance of education in us, they reminded us of the blessings we had and the impact of being kind to everyone.

I grew up playing basketball, baseball, tennis, and soccer. Basketball remained my strongest passion, which intensified when I attended North Carolina State University and cheered at all the great (and not so great) basketball games. I began volunteering in middle school and continued through college, where I built a long-standing foundation of community service through leadership positions, interfaith programs, working with City of Raleigh youth programs, and a dedication to social justice.

All of this prepared me for bringing my experiences into the government arena, to help bridge the gap between the policies created and the people served. My background, my community, and my love for my hometown inspired me to run for Raleigh City Council.

As a Muslim Woman, I know I have to work at least 5 times harder than other people to be respected and to have influence in my leadership positions. Both politics and my educational endeavors are very male-dominated fields. I am usually the only Muslim at the table and sometimes the first Muslim people have interacted with. I struggle with staying true to my feminine side while still being assertive and managing different initiatives. I've learned to listen to people, to be patient, and to always (regardless of how mad someone might make me) be empathetic to others' needs. This is where my faith plays a huge role. The Qur'an says, "Those who spend in prosperity and adversity, and those who suppress anger and pardon men; and Allah loves those who do good (3:134, Kamal Omar). Islam taught me how to be compassionate and to always treat people well regardless of who they are, what they believe, and what they might think of me.

I attribute my successes to my compassion for people. The hardest part is dealing with people who hold stereotypes or hatred towards Muslims. Dealing with constant anti-Muslim rhetoric and having a President who promotes it is tough. It is hard to stay kind toward people who hate you for wearing a piece of cloth on your head, but I know this stems from ignorance and not being educated about Islam other than through the negative rhetoric the media spews. It's common for people to see my hijab (headscarf) and assume that I live a life of oppression, where only extrication from my religion can "liberate" me. I'm consistently baffled by this. I see myself as a strong, empowered young Muslim-American woman who has overcome the bigotry, ignorance, and racism that attempted to make me feel ashamed of my Islamic beliefs and values.

Islam came with a revolutionary message that uplifts women's status to claim equality in stature and worship. Remarkably, these rights came at a time when no one was protesting or rallying about the mistreatment of women. Only a century ago, and after fierce fighting from determined women in the Suffrage movement, was the 19th Amendment to the U.S. Constitution adopted, granting American women the right to vote. In fact, many of the rights that Islam honored women with more than 1,400 years ago were not granted to women in the West until the late 18th and 19th centuries.

The Qur'an put an end to inequality by granting women spiritual, intellectual, economic, and social rights equal to, if not more than, men. Prophet Muhammad explicitly taught gender equality and took numerous concrete measures to profoundly improve the status and role of women.

My religion is the reason I am who I am today. It is the reason I've been empowered to lead a life fighting for social justice, and fighting not just for my community but for all communities. I am a tenacious, strong-willed individual who has control over my life because of Islam's portrayal of the way society should view women, and the way I view myself.

♔☭❀ॐ✿✝☾

Donna Hakimian *is the Bahá'í Chaplain at Harvard University and the Bahá'í Spiritual Advisor at Northeastern University. She is also a graduate resident advisor at iHouse, an undergraduate living-learning community at the Massachusetts Institute of Technology, which focuses on international development and service. Prior to this, she served as the Representative for Gender Equality and the Advancement of Women at the U.S. Bahá'í Office of Public Affairs. Ms. Hakimian holds an Ed.M. from the Harvard Graduate School of Education, an M.A. in Women's Studies from the University of Toronto, and a B.A. from McGill University. Her interests include health and spirituality, international cuisine and music, and ceramic art.*

Beyond Bias

When you close your eyes and imagine an economist, what do you see? Something to that effect was asked in a newspaper article discussing implicit bias, and in particular Janet Yellen, Chair of the Federal Reserve from 2014–2018. The article outlined how despite many of our best efforts, exposure to stereotypes and deep-seated beliefs about what leadership looks like colors how female economists are treated. Reading this article was both a moment of awareness for me and a moment of sadness for all the little girls *and* little boys who are denied the possibility of knowing a more inclusive world, and in turn, knowing all the possibilities for themselves.

Next, I turn to the memory of one of my heroines, Bahíyyih Khánum, the daughter of the Prophet Founder of the Bahá'í Faith, Bahá'u'lláh. A leader in early Bahá'í history, she experienced years of difficult persecution and exile along with her father and the rest of her family. A petite woman, with deep, penetrating eyes, photographs of her evoke a peace, steadfastness, beauty, and tenacity that since my childhood have inspired me.

I present both of these examples to explore whether leadership can be conceived of differently and more inclusively. To allow for a different, broader embodiment of what it means to lead. This is not to say that one group should be replaced with another, but rather to invite all, with their various life experiences, gifts, and potentialities, to shine forth and be heard.

This has particular implications for the gendered ways in which society brands certain attributes as masculine and others as feminine and, sadly, also equates some qualities as strong and others as weak. Gender inequality more broadly has had ruinous consequences in the social, political, and personal realms. Consider the disproportionate impact gender violence has on women and girls, or how this is reflected in the official positions held by women and men, or even the ways laws are written and enacted.

Rather than fall defeated to the dizzying number of challenges humanity faces in this regard, I take heart in the following idea from Bahá'í Scripture: "Women and men have been and will always be equal in the sight of God."[2]

I also return to the memory of Bahíyyih Khánum and draw inspiration from her legacy. At a point in Bahá'í history she assumed headship of the Faith. This was within a largely gender-segregated societal context, in which women were seen as holding a far lower status than that of men. In fact, even doing historical research on women during this time period is a challenge.

In my opinion the essence of progress will happen when each of our unique potentialities as members of the human race are honored and welcomed. A large part of this is reconceiving leadership and service, in all the forms they take, to include and value both the feminine and the masculine elements of society.

---

[2]Bahá'u'lláh, from a tablet translated from the Persian and Arabic, quoted in *Women: Extracts from the Writings of Bahá'u'lláh, 'Abdu'l-Bahá, Shoghi Effendi and the Universal House of Justice*, (Bahá'í Public Trust, 1986), 26.

One of my favorite quotes about Bahíyyih Khánum describes her in the following terms: "...as she would not lock away her small treasures, neither would she store up her wisdom and her riches of experience. In her, experience left no bitter ash. Her flame transmuted all of life, even its crude and base particles, into gold. And this gold she spent."[3]

Elsewhere it is written, "For her love was unconditioned, could penetrate disguise and see hunger behind the mask of fury, and she knew that the most brutal self is secretly hoping to find gentleness in another."[4]

Bahíyyih Khánum's exemplary way of living and being, from the most personal of individual interactions to complex administrative roles, has inspired me to improve my own spiritual path. This takes the shape of my striving to embody compassionate understanding and love, even in moments of difficulty. It helps me to see the spiritual connection that all beings share, and inspires me to live generously with this vision of unity always at the forefront. Her example has helped me to be gentler with others and myself.

Leadership is not simply the way anyone, whether man or woman, is portrayed in their public life. Rather, leadership is this public role *combined* with the ability to be loving, forgiving, and kind. This is what these quotes embody to me, that Bahíyyih Khánum lived, and which my faith has set for me as an example. An everyday struggle, no doubt, but a pursuit that I feel is well worth the effort and has thus far yielded beautiful fruits.

Ⓟ☯✻ॐ☸✝☪

Reverend J. Dana Trent *is a graduate of Duke University Divinity School and is an award-winning author, speaker, minister, and teacher. She teaches World Religions at Wake Technical Community College in Raleigh, North Carolina. Her academic and research interests include Christian meditation and sabbath-keeping in a 24/7 world. Dana is the author of four books.* Saffron Cross: The Unlikely Story of How a Christian Minister Married a Hindu Monk *chronicles her interfaith*

---

[3]Marjory Morten, "Bahíyyih Khánum," *The Bahá'í World,* Vol. 5 (1932-1934): 181–85.

[4]Morten, 181–85.

marriage to Fred Eaker. Her latest book, Dessert First: Preparing for Death While Savoring Life, *explores her work as an end-of-life chaplain and grief guru, and delves into multi-faith perspectives on death, grief, and the afterlife.*

Women's Voices

Women run the church, and they have forever. No one hesitates to ask women to do things, and everyone knows that women are the backbone of the church; but in terms of having power and voice and leadership, they are not recognized for all their service.

Women were present at Jesus' resurrection. They were the first to witness the resurrection and the first to spread the news, so they were the first evangelists. Because Christianity hinges on this resurrection story, the fact that the women were present at the tomb is integral to the role they play in the ministry today and historically.

What is reflected in the gospel is not reflected in the church. As of 2012 women were still just 11 percent of clergy ordained in the entire Christian church, in all denominations, according to Mark Chaves's book *Ordaining Women.*[5] Just a few denominations have women in leadership positions, such as bishop. So although the gospel narrative is strong, and there are many strong women in the Bible, it does not reflect the reality of the role of women.

The disconnect has a lot to do with society and culture, and with the fact that women's voices in scripture show up considerably less than men's voices. Although we have these wonderful narratives and stories, and we have a trickle of women's voices, it's not the majority voice. In the Southern Baptist tradition in which I was raised, the *Baptist Faith & Message* says that according to scripture women cannot be in leadership roles.[6] We use this document across the denomination to set up a system in which we won't allow women to teach male children above the age of thirteen, or to have any leadership roles including deacon and pastor.

We use scripture to justify it, and there have been atrocities committed using those kinds of texts to justify terrible actions and

---

[5]Mark Chaves, *Ordaining Women: Culture and Conflict in Religious Organizations* (Cambridge, MA: Harvard University Press, 1999).

[6]*The Baptist Faith and Message 2000,* http://www.sbc.net/bfm2000/bfm2000.asp .

oppression of people for centuries. Any document that oppresses others is not the gospel. The gospel is love; it's going to the margins; it's healing, it's service, it's "the first shall be last, the last shall be first" (Mt. 20:16). In some ways it's counter-intuitive. It turns everything upside-down. If we're going to get women heard, we've got to flip the current system.

My personal experience was one of being affirmed in terms of ordination, but not encouraged to consider a pastoral leadership role. My home church ordained me because they knew I would never seek out a senior pastor position. I would never be a threat.

When I came to seminary, my placement was at Binkley Baptist Church in Chapel Hill, North Carolina. They embraced my gifts and gave me leadership. My last year of seminary I was an interim Christian Educator because someone was out on maternity leave. It felt so affirming that they trusted me with this job.

I was baptized by a female clergy woman at Binkley Baptist. What a joy and honor it was to be baptized by a woman. I remember it being one of the most profound moments of my life, especially because I was in the arms of Dr. Linda Jordan, Binkley's first female senior pastor. I felt particularly nurtured and cared for. Those are the gifts that women bring to the table, in addition to many other gifts. I don't want to over-generalize, but those are the gifts of devotion. Those are the gifts of the gospel. Those are the gifts of love.

Men in the church have an obligation to mentor young clergy women, to make a way for them, give them voice, to give them the pulpit. It will have to be the men who are willing to say to the parish: We are going to make a way for a female clergy person. That's what we need Christian pastors, male and female, to be doing—putting women in the pulpit.

Women's voices are being heard more on a national level, but not necessarily in the pulpit. There are people who are hungry to hear women's voices from the pulpit, especially those who welcome and affirm LBGTQIA+ persons and promote inclusion.

I'm not the kind of woman who typically speaks out, but I'm realizing that I cannot keep quiet. For me it's going to be through writing, being edgier, being louder, being more direct, being confrontational, being strong, being empowered—because the voices that oppress women are loud, they're confrontational, and they're empowered. Those of us who are more open-minded want to say, "Oh, I hear where you're coming from and I'm seeking to understand your point of view." We can still have that, but we also have to draw a line and say, "But you have to hear my voice, too."

ॐ❀ॐ☥✝☾

Fred Eaker lived as a Hindu monk between the ages of 22 and 27. In 2005, he was ordained into the tradition of Caitanya Vaishnavism by Swami B.V. Tripurari. In 2010, Fred married J. Dana Trent, an ordained, female Southern Baptist who subsequently published a book about their interfaith marriage entitled Saffron Cross. *Fred is currently an Assistant Director of Technology Services at North Carolina State University. As a result of his monastic experience and his coursework for an M.A. in Liberal Studies concentrating on identity, ethics, and social justice, Fred is passionate about imagining a future without exploitative economic arrangements fueled by white supremacy, and instead building Gandhian communities of care as an alternative social arrangement.*

A Better Way

Hinduism can be very complex and nuanced, so we have several different concepts of the divine feminine. We have a very prominent God the mother concept in Hinduism. She has many names: Durga, Kali, Lakshmi, Parvati, Radha; and she has all the qualities that a good mother has—very nurturing, protective, and invincible. We also have a concept of the mother of God, kind of like Mary, called Yoshodama. She has a particular form of love for God that's very beautiful, and we believe you should actually worship her. It's got some nice parallels with Catholicism.

We have in my tradition a very peculiar way of thinking about the divine feminine. God, "he," is actually controlled by "her," because he loves her so much. He has an existential crisis and thinks, "Am I God? I want to worship her, but everybody is worshipping me," and it causes a lot of confusion. Our conclusion is that it's better to worship her and become her servant. So we have multiple ways of thinking about the divine feminine.

There are stories of prominent women teachers in our line. Women can be gurus, but broadly speaking, there's strong patriarchy still present in Hinduism. The female monk that lived at the monastery with us was a leader. She wasn't the kind of person who put herself forward, but everyone knew her level of advancement and her level of devotion. She was very much respected, and I personally have a tremendous amount of admiration for her. She helped me a lot when I was in the monastery. I saw visitors come to the monastery and ignore her or insult her in some subtle way. She's one of the more spiritually advanced people that I know. The teaching in Hinduism is that it doesn't matter what kind of body you have. It's really all about this heartfelt, soul-oriented devotion to God, and that can happen in any form of life.

I am both proud and fortunate to be married to a strong female faith leader. On several occasions, I have traveled with Dana to assist and support her as she leads church retreats and gives challenging sermons, even to congregations outside of her own faith tradition. Dana not only delivers impassioned messages for multi-faith understanding and introspective, faith-filled approaches to social justice, but I have also watched her connect with people in very profound ways, often moving them to tears as they reconnect to their faith and their community. Dana has gifts and strengths that are very difficult for me to cultivate, gifts that are either in short supply or devalued in our current sociocultural environment. The fact that I have an opportunity to support such a person adds great meaning to my life. It also provides me with a chance to use my socially-constructed privilege as a white male to support a minority voice and encourage social change.

In my particular tradition of Hinduism, we are encouraged to practice in a way that cultivates the ability to perceive the teachings of the guru in all situations. My marriage to Dana is a situation in which I am grateful to witness that religious and spiritual insight is not determined by gender, that the marginalized are a source of critical insight, and that strong relationships bound by selfless service to each other are at the core of what it means to be a decent human.

I would like to see women in more leadership positions. I think women tend to have a much more inclusive style when they're in leadership, and they encourage participatory decision-making. We need institutions both religious and secular where we have more participatory decision-making. All religious institutions should set examples for the rest of society, and I think it goes back to how you design your institutions to be more inclusive and to include more people in the decision-making process. If Hindu communities, and Christian communities, could design themselves in such a way that when people from secular society come to a temple or a church and actually see a different way of doing things, a different way of organizing, a different way of relating to each other, that could be a huge lesson to secular society. Any religious community has an opportunity to show that there's a better way. All traditions have the tools in their scriptures to do that.

ॐ☸࿉☬†☪

Reflection Questions

• Are there particular scriptures or holy texts in your faith tradition that speak about women's roles? How have they been used within your religion's organizations to limit or empower women seeking leadership roles?

• Are there examples of strong women within your religion's history who inspire you, as Bahíyyih Khánum inspired Donna Hakimian? What do their examples teach you about your faith?

• Have you seen and known women in top leadership roles in your religious institution? If so, how have they influenced your spiritual growth?

• J. Dana Trent believes more women's voices need to be heard in Christian pulpits. In what ways have you experienced religion used to oppress women or limit women's roles and voices? In what ways have you experienced religion as a means of empowering women?

• Fred Eaker writes about the concepts of the feminine divine in his tradition of Hinduism. In your religious tradition, does the divine have a gender? How does the way you conceive of the divine's gender influence your understanding of human gender roles?

- What steps could your religious institution take to include more women in decision-making? What are some ways you could facilitate this on a local or a national level?

Interfaith Conflict and Extremism

Diane's Introduction

I felt compelled to create this book because so many terrible things are done in the name of religion, including my own Christian faith. When we do not understand and empathize with one another, the negative actions of a few religious extremists become the only lens through which we view an entire group of believers. Such stereotypes make it easier to then justify and continue the cycle of violence against one another.

Turning on the news might lead us to believe the world is experiencing an unprecedented spike in religiously-motivated violence. We can easily point a finger at extremists from other religions who commit atrocities in the name of their faith. Hateful acts inspired by religious beliefs have become inseparable from the practice of that religion itself, in the minds of many fearful onlookers. This, however, is not solely a modern phenomenon. Every major world religion has ugly incidents of violence woven throughout history. Stories of wars and violence against outsiders co-exist with teachings on acceptance and peace within many religions' holy texts, and so believers of all kinds must carefully examine their scriptures and history to make sense of such contradictions. We all have skeletons in our ancestral faith closets, as well as modern faith cousins whose extreme, violent behavior does not represent our own beliefs and practices. In addition, religion often becomes intertwined with greed, power, politics, and nationalism, so that extremists' motivations may be a messy mix of many factors, of which faith is only one small part.

Christian history is littered with crusaders, klansmen, and even callous missionaries whose desire to promote and protect their religion's ideals (as they understood them) blinded them to the humanity of people they saw as "the other." Christian extremists have long found ways to justify hateful acts, in spite of Jesus' example throughout the Bible's New Testament. Jesus repeatedly offered love, healing, and acceptance to people his peers rejected. Jesus taught his followers to "turn the other cheek" in the face of violence (Matthew 5:39), and proclaimed "blessed are the peacemakers" (Matthew 5:9). When Jesus was about to be arrested and sentenced to death, one of his disciples tried to protect him by cutting off the ear of a soldier. Jesus said, "Put your sword back into its place; for all who take the sword will perish by the sword" (Matthew 26:52). Jesus chose to submit to persecution rather than respond with violence.

Submission is also a key theme in Islam. The ideal of Jihad, which many misunderstand as a holy war, in fact teaches Muslims to continue the struggle to practice their faith even in the face of persecution and oppression. While this can apply to both internal and external struggles, armed struggle against persecution is to be used only as a last resort. The Qur'an teaches: "Be steadfast witnesses for Allah in equity, and let not hatred of any people seduce you that ye deal not justly" (5:8, M.M. Pickthall).

The Middle East has long witnessed the struggle of Christians, Muslims, and Jews—which share common ancestors—to live peaceably on lands considered holy to all three. The Jewish people, in particular, have been cast as outsiders and scapegoats in many parts of the world throughout their history, justifying violence against and by those who would keep the Jewish faith and culture alive. At the heart of Judaism, however, is the commandment, "You shall not murder," (Exodus 20:13) and the desire to seek a world in which "the wolf shall live with the lamb" and no one shall "hurt or destroy on all my holy mountain" (Isaiah 11:6–9). Both ancient and modern Jewish prophets cast a vision of a peaceful world, such as the one articulated by Isaiah: "they shall beat their swords into plowshares, and their spears into pruning hooks; nation shall not lift up sword against nation, neither shall they learn war any more" (Isaiah 2:4).

In Southeast Asia, too, the confluence of religions has frequently led to conflict among neighbors. Yet the teachings of Buddhism and Hinduism promote tolerance and treating all living beings with respect.

As the stories which follow remind us, persecution of people because of their faith has very personal consequences and can be especially devastating to multi-faith families. In reality, all of us, in our global family, are harmed when we use faith as an excuse to justify the mistreatment of others for our own benefit.

Ⓠ☯✳︎ॐ�at☪︎⃰

Ayat Husseini *is an International Affairs and Anthropology/Sociology major at Lafayette College in Easton, Pennsylvania. She was born in Beirut, Lebanon, and at the age of three moved to Astoria, New York, where she has lived ever since. She is a daughter, sister, student, activist, reader, writer, volunteer, and community builder. When she is not writing papers and attending social justice–related events, she is cooking, singing, or planning a research project.*

Seventeen Years, Two Months, and Ten Days

Anyone who knows me well knows I start most arguments with "as a Lebanese-American, Muslim, immigrant woman..." It's a new habit, but I have always worn my identity on my sleeve. When you have such an incredibly politicized identity the way I do, it's hard not to pick up on the fact that not everyone accepts every part of you. By the time I was seven years old, I had already heard so many jokes about Islamic extremism, and seen my mother harassed so many times in public because of her hijab, I had made up my mind that I would not wear the hijab. A part of me rejected my Muslim identity.

I was three years and nine days old on September 11, 2001. I was 5,627 miles away from the Twin Towers when they came down, and yet fifteen years later, a peer told me I should have been capable of preventing this terrorist attack.

I was six years, ten months, and eleven days old on July 13, 2006. I found myself 5,611 miles away from Beirut Rafic Hariri International Airport when it was bombed by Israeli forces.

I was told by my American peers that the war was a byproduct of Islamic extremism and that any other opinion meant I was less American. Because my identity is split between a number of different places, I am always expected to take one side or the other. Regardless of the opinion I take, I am still standing directly in the line of fire. I was never given the opportunity to form an opinion on the 2006 War and yet, when I returned to Lebanon seven years after the conflict had been resolved, I was told that I was too American and too Westernized. I was left stranded, sitting alone on the hyphen of Lebanese and American, between Muslim and American.

I was seventeen years, two months, and ten days old on November 12, 2015. I was 5,613 miles away from Bourj al-Barajneh, Lebanon, when a car bomb killed 43 bystanders and injured more than 200. I was seventeen years, two months, and ten days old on November 12, 2015. I was 3,618 miles from Paris, France, when bombings took the lives of 129 innocent people and injured more than 350. The entire Western world stood in solidarity with France on this day, but because Lebanon seemed to be used to car bombings, this attack was not considered important enough for Western attention. While both attacks were claimed by the same Islamic extremist group, the War on Terror had made terrorism a front that the Western world must fight against only when Western lives are at stake.

I found out that night just why I had resented my Muslim identity for so long. Islamic extremism is not a fight between the Muslim East and the American West. It is not the kind of fight where you can clearly mark out both sides by referring to country names or geographic locations. I realized this war is between extremism in all of it forms and all of those who oppose it. Somewhere along the lines, the story was misconstrued, allowing the new narrative labeling the "sides" as all Muslims versus all non-Muslims.

That night I realized that when religious identities are politicized, the way mine has been, the carnage, casualties, and despair cannot be reconciled with politics. I've learned that when extremism becomes the first connotation that others have regarding your religion, the only way to combat that is with kindness.

I was three, four, five, six, seven, eight, nine, ten, eleven, twelve, thirteen, fourteen, fifteen, sixteen, seventeen, and eighteen years old when I watched my mother treat with kindness those who treated her with hostility because of her hijab. I was always just a few feet away.

When these things happen, I remember that this narrative we are being told is not the true story. I remember that the conflict is not between faiths but rather between the good and the evil, and those two groups are not so simply distinguishable. I remember that "Indeed, Allah enjoins justice, and the doing of good to others" (16.90, author's paraphrase).

I am eighteen years, ten months, and twenty-nine days old today, July 31, 2017. I still wear my identity on my sleeve. I still don't wear the hijab, but I am so incredibly proud to be Muslim, and when the time comes, I plan to. I celebrate my own identity and all of its parts. I am kind and loving, and I work through all avenues I see before me to seek interreligious understanding and to show others the truth about extremism. My name is Ayat Husseini, and I look to my mother and my Holy Book to inspire kindness, hope, and understanding.

ॐ☬✡☸✝☪

Joshua Jeffreys *lives with his wife, Amy, and newborn son, Marc, in Richmond, Virginia, where he serves at the University of Richmond as the Jewish Chaplain and Director of Religious Life. As a Jewish educator, administrator, and interfaith leader, Josh has worked in various Jewish community organizations since high school and now works to provide opportunities for individuals of all faith backgrounds to engage across lines of difference through worship, community engagement, cultural and religious education, and more. A native of New Jersey, Josh received his undergraduate degree in Jewish Studies from Rutgers University in 2013, a Masters in Business Administration from the University of Richmond in 2019, and is currently studying toward rabbinic ordination through ALEPH: The Alliance for Jewish Renewal.*

Tree of Life: Fighting Antisemitism through
Remembrance and Radical Love

I woke up on Saturday, October 27, 2018, a little later than usual. My wife and I had guests in town, and I made coffee for the group as I would for myself on any normal day. But it was not a normal day. As the coffee brewed, I checked the latest news on Twitter—the millennial version of reading the Saturday morning newspaper—and was devastated by the still-unfolding string of events that would eventually leave 11 Jews dead at the Tree of Life synagogue in Pittsburgh, Pennsylvania.

Our day continued as planned with brunch, a tour of Richmond, and visits to a few local breweries. My wife occasionally inquired if I was ok, and I responded that everything was fine. The truth is I was anything but fine, but I was still processing the developing news out of Pittsburgh and couldn't find the words to describe the mixture of pain, sadness, anger, and growing terror I felt in response to the deadliest attack against Jews in American history. "Fine" would have to do.

On Monday I returned to work, where I spent the day consoling and supporting Jewish college students. The day stood in stark contrast to the previous Friday evening, the last time I had been with many of those same students before the shooting, when we had gathered to celebrate Shabbat as a community through festive meal and prayer. In that way, we were not very different from those at Tree of Life who had been observing Shabbat, in prayer with God and community, as Jews everywhere have done for thousands of years. But unlike Jews everywhere, their Shabbat observance was interrupted by a hateful and violent manifestation of the same antisemitism Jews have known throughout our history.

As I continue to reflect on the Tree of Life shooting, engaging with both my personal emotions and those of the Jewish students I am charged with supporting, I recall my formative years as a young Jew, constantly reminded of the atrocities committed against my ancestors simply because they chose to live Jewish lives. So many of our holidays—Passover, Hanukkah, Purim, Tisha B'Av, and Yom HaShoah (just to name a few)—deal with the oppression or attempted destruction of Jews. I spent countless hours in my Jewish studies courses learning the history of antisemitism and its effects on Jews and our collective psyche. While I now understand that my tradition entails so much more, the memory of my peoples' oppression became a central part of my understanding of what it meant to be Jewish. The act of remembering became my most important Jewish responsibility, "Never again" the most vital commandment.

However, I am a straight, white, cisgender male. Despite some years of physical and emotional hardships, I remain able-bodied. Surrounding many years of financial struggle, I enjoyed and now enjoy again socioeconomic security. No matter how much I understood regarding the litany of injustices against Jews that *logically* followed unchecked antisemitic rhetoric, I regret that I never fully comprehended this lesson. Not because I didn't believe what I was taught, but because my lived experience as a Reform Jew in America with considerable privilege made such disasters inconceivable. The admonition to remember—*zakhor*—so that a Holocaust would never again happen was deeply ingrained in me, but I still failed to understand *viscerally* how the Holocaust was possible in the first place. Though my eyes were open, I did not truly see how such a tragedy could be repeated. But on Saturday, October 27, I saw.

The loss of 11 beautiful souls during the Tree of Life shooting triggered for me an intergenerational trauma that Jews—young and old alike—have carried with us for millennia. A list of massacres committed against the Jewish people from Pharaoh's Egypt to Nazi Germany. Atrocities that suddenly seem all too real for many American Jews—myself included.

What I knew cerebrally but never fully internalized is that memory *is* central to Judaism. As Jews are commanded 36 times (far more than any other commandment) in the Torah: "Love the stranger, for you were strangers in the land of Egypt" (Deuteronomy 10:19). Remembering is only half our responsibility; acting because of that memory is the far more important piece.

The Tree of Life massacre was a stark reminder of the work left to do to end not just antisemitism and violence against Jews domestically (which has increased rapidly in the last several years) and abroad, but the oppression of all strangers. Now is the time for me to love radically. To actively and inclusively love the stranger, the widow, the orphan, the poor, and the sick. To love and support those most marginalized and oppressed in my community: people of color, members of the LGBTQ community, women, religious minorities, those of other nationalities, and those of no nation. Only through such an extreme form of love, informed by my memory as a Jew, can I claim to have fulfilled the most pressing commandment of ensuring "Never Again" is not a hollow promise.

✡︎☪︎✴︎ॐ☯︎✝︎☾

Deborah Miller *grew up in a small North Carolina coastal town. After graduating from Campbell University and North Carolina State University, she spent her career in human services, serving as the Executive Director of Wake Enterprises, Inc., in Raleigh, North Carolina, for 14 years. In addition to lapidary arts, she enjoys spending time with her grandchildren and writing poetry. Her first book,* Remnants of Strawberry Blonde, *was published in 2013. She is editing a manuscript for a second book.*

Things Like That Don't Happen Anymore

My parents' struggle to live and love in difficult circumstances changed and challenged me. My dad was Jewish, my mother, Protestant, and we lived in a coastal North Carolina town. Dad was as comfortable in a Christian church as in a synagogue. Before meeting my mother, he visited the South with an employee from my grandfather's business. He went to church with him and discovered the Christian faith. Dad knew the words to Christian hymns better than deacons in the front pew at the Baptist church. Though he found himself unwelcome in places of worship in town, his money was always welcome.

For many years, my parents lived without encountering much antisemitic behavior. Some people remarked that my brother (injured in birth, with forceps) was disabled because my mother "married a Jew." Most antisemitism was in church sermons—especially at Easter, "when the Jews killed Christ." One church we attended asked members to donate a pipe organ for their sanctuary. When my parents offered them an organ, the church leadership explained that they would not take a tangible item from a Jew, but they would be okay with cash. When dad went to church with us, the minister always went off message to say something negative about Jews.

In the late 1960s, my parents left town. The skeleton of a dead cow was hoisted up on our furniture store one night after we went home. The attached note said, "We have picked you clean, you can leave town now." My dad's financial records had been altered; money in his accounts was missing, and there was nothing we could do about it. No local attorney would take our case. Eventually, we found an attorney, but he couldn't get anywhere. The state could not force the financial institution to disclose the amount of money in my parents' accounts because they were a private entity. Dad was unable to file his taxes, because the bank said that since the accounts were part of a lawsuit, they couldn't disclose what was in them.

One day a man questioned my parents about my knowledge of their business problems. When my mother replied that I was aware of what had transpired, he said it would be a "shame if something happened to your daughter while she was away at college." That was the end of the conflict. My parents signed anything put in front of them.

Mom later experienced a depressive episode from which she never recovered. The psychiatrist chuckled as he told me that my mother believed water had been put in the gasoline tank of her car, phone lines had been cut inexplicably, money in her accounts had disappeared, and someone had put a cow skeleton on her roof. I said, "Yes, that part is true." He sternly told me, "things like that don't happen anymore."

They moved, and dad started life over at sixty as a locker room attendant in a country club, making minimum wage. He was fluent in several languages, had a phenomenal memory, and was a "character" in every sense of the word. My parents lived on that minimum wage salary, and dad saved his tips. He met people who were stockbrokers and carefully listened as they talked about investments, pouring every extra cent into the stock market. In five years, his investments generated enough money to support him for the next thirty years.

Mom passed away at the age of seventy—too young. Certainly, stress was a contributing factor. My father outlived those who

ruined his life, with the exception of one, the main instigator. I
think about him sometimes, but like my parents I have little room
in my life for anger.

Though dad couldn't be a part of the churches where I grew
up, he was never far from faith. I used to slip into my parents'
bedroom and listen to dad pray in Hebrew and English, as he
recited the prayers of his fathers and prayed for us. My husband
and I wanted our children to grow up in a church where everyone
is welcome—where people can explore issues of faith without fear
of intimidation or exclusion; where we are responsible for the care
of one another, regardless of income, social status, or any other
differences.

My dad died in 2014, at ninety-eight years old. It took a long time
to say "goodbye" to my father, to put in perspective circumstances
that bound us together in that town. I tell my parents' story as a
reminder that prejudice and discrimination are real, and we are
responsible for the lives around us. While none of us may share
the same experiences, we all know about love and loss.

☬☸✡🕉☩†☪

*Tahil Sharma is an interfaith activist based in Los Angeles who was
born to a Hindu father and a Sikh mother. Following the Oak Creek,
Wisconsin, shooting at a Sikh temple in 2012, Tahil became involved in
efforts for interfaith literacy and social justice and has been doing this
work professionally for the past seven years. Tahil is the Faith Outreach
Manager for Brave New Films, a social justice documentary organization
that empowers communities and teaches civic participation. Tahil also
serves as one of three Interfaith Ministers in Residence for the Episcopal
Diocese of Los Angeles and as the Los Angeles Coordinator for Sadhana:
A Coalition of Progressive Hindus.*

Family Bonds

I was born to a Hindu father and a Sikh mother who gave birth
to me and raised me in the United States. I was brought up in an
inclusive and supportive home where diversity and pluralism were
affirmed by my faith traditions, and were essential in shaping my

worldview to focus on the principles of non-violence, compassion, and mutual respect. Hinduism and Sikhism helped me learn that differences in perspective are not bad things. They've taught me that understanding the world and God cannot be simplified to a single and exclusive point of view. Imagine the cognitive dissonance that put my entire world into question when the fringe of my faith communities showed the worst of humankind. It led me to ask how my existence heals the wounds of eroding relationships and a coexisting society in decay.

The year 1984 brings back the memories of George Orwell's dystopian novel to some people. That story might have served as foreshadowing for a real state of chaos and oppression that unfolded in my parents' homeland of India. It was also the year that my family was joined through the union of my parents as husband and wife. Their marriage was met with great reluctance and condemnation. My mom's side of the family feared her adjustment from army to civilian life, and members of my dad's family could not accept a marriage occurring "outside of the faith," but everyone made it work and completed the necessary customs for their respective religious traditions. Knowing the obstacles that would await them after their wedding, my parents' union was rooted in their love for each other and their mutual respect and appreciation for each other's worldview.

After months of mistreatment from my father's family, my parents moved back into my maternal grandparents' home. Little did they realize that worse chaos would ensue and test the bond of their interfaith marriage.

The year 1984 was also the year of Operation Blue Star, a week-long Indian Army operation against a group of armed Sikh men who had sought refuge in the *Harmandir Sahib* complex, more popularly known as the Golden Temple of Amritsar, in rebellion against the government for the various crises that plagued the state of Punjab. Gunshots and bombs resulted in the defacement of the *Akal Takht Sahib*, one of the most significant and sacred institutions to the Sikh community and a major construction of the Golden Temple complex, and the subsequent death of army officers, the armed men within the complex, and hundreds of innocent civilians. This was just the beginning.

October of the same year brought both my worldviews to the battlefield as two Sikh bodyguards assassinated the Prime Minister, Indira Gandhi. Her death resulted in genocidal pogroms against the Sikh community instigated by right-wing Hindu groups across India, supported by the Indian National Congress, the party of the Prime Minister. Sikh men were taken from homes and stabbed, shot, beheaded, and given "tire garlands." Women were beaten, raped, and killed merely for belonging to the Sikh faith tradition. My mother and her family were immediately sheltered by the many people who had come to know them, across the spectrum of religious and secular perspective. My father joined other young people in protecting various neighborhoods by standing in the way of mobs wanting to invade properties and public spaces in search of Sikh families. Unfortunately, the same protection could not be extended to my grandfather, a retired Brigadier General in the Engineers Corps of the Indian Army, who went missing for three days after being beaten by a frenzy of Hindu ruffians and almost being thrown into a burning truck. On his return home, he was so battered and bruised that it took forty-five minutes to wash his turban, to remove the blood soaked up from his head injuries.

The lessons from what my family went through serve as a framework for the work that I do today. My grandfather's ability to recover and retain a heart of mercy after such inflictions for just being Sikh continue to motivate my work for peace between communities. Our compassion cannot be limited to what we are comfortable with and what we are aware of because the entire universe is our family. We continue with a relentless optimism that we can serve as beacons of hope and justice in a world that is fragile and weary.

The powerful bond between my parents demonstrates a real need to understand fear and ignorance at its core. The way they understood and respected each other's differences and imperfections to create their own perfection showed me that my very existence is essential in educating and advocating for justice. I cannot build a bridge because I am a bridge. My existence refutes the idea that communities in conflict will remain in conflict. The potential to sustain peace and equity comes from our ability to change minds and hearts that may think otherwise. You shouldn't help others because you know them. You should help others because they need help. If the arc does not bend toward justice, we must bend it ourselves.

✟☸✡ॐ☸✿✝☾

Glun Siu *lives in Raleigh, North Carolina, where he is a member and Elder of St. Paul's Christian Church. He and his wife, Jum, have five children. Glun was born in a small village in the central highlands of Viet Nam. He is Montagnard, an indigenous people who helped the Americans during the Viet Nam War. He came to the United States as a refugee in 2002, and became a U.S. citizen in 2016. He enjoys playing volleyball with his friends, and he works as a custodian at a local high school.*

A Better Life

Editor's Note from Diane: I am Glun's pastor. He shared this story with me about how becoming a Christian was deeply intertwined with empowering him to organize for the rights of his people. The persecution he faced probably had more to do with his activism than his faith, but without the spiritual and practical resources he found in Christianity, he would not have been moved to stand up against the oppression of the Montagnard people.

When I was a baby, my parents passed away. I lived with my brother, but he did not like me much. I did not go to school. When I was just five years old, I took care of my niece and nephew, and I was a farmer, too. My life was difficult. I had no house. I had nothing. I married my wife, but we had no food. The government from Hanoi came and had money you could apply to borrow. I said I wanted to borrow some money, so I could start a farm. They said no, this money is only for rich people to borrow. I was very angry.

I first learned about God when I got married. I had seen people who were Christians, but I didn't know anything about them. People in my village prayed to the mountains and the water. Older people killed chickens and sprinkled their blood on the ground. I knew some people who became Christians, and they spoke with kindness. They spoke to my heart. They stopped drinking and took care of their families. They helped people whose lives were difficult. I wanted Christ to come into my heart. I didn't want my heart to be angry.

I had never seen my language written before I saw the Bible. The

Christians showed me the sounds written out in Jarai. Before, I didn't know how to read and write. I wanted to learn from them. The government became angry because my friends and cousins and I began to learn about Christianity, and we began to learn to read our own language.

When people in my village began forming a group to learn Christianity, the government thought we were organizing to take back our land. They didn't want us to get together like that. They called me into a government office in a city far away. When I went, they put a handgun on the table in front of me and warned me not to continue. I said if I do something bad, you leave me alone; but if I want to learn how to be good and help my friends and family, to not be so angry, you threaten me. My life is very difficult. I don't have a house, I don't have food, I have nothing, and the government would not even lend me money to improve my life. That's why I became a Christian, so I would not be so angry. They told me they would be watching me, but they let me go home.

More and more people came to my house to pray and learn about being Christian. We met at night, in secret. I went to the nearby towns to talk about Christianity and to talk about Montagnard rights. A second time, people from the government came to my village to interrogate me.

My friend's father worked for the government. He saw a piece of paper with my name and my friends' names on it. It was a list of people they planned to arrest or kill. My friend ran to my house to tell me I had to leave. I called all my friends to tell them, and we decided we had to go away. Someone knew about a village just across the border in Cambodia where we could go. When we left, we didn't know if we would live or die, we just ran. Ninety-nine people went. We were in the jungle for 12 days, without food. One man died while we were crossing a river. The Vietnamese army came after us and fired their guns, but we escaped. When things were difficult in the jungle, I prayed, and God took care of us.

In Cambodia, we stayed in a United Nations camp for nine months. They fed us, but not enough. We couldn't go out, because we were afraid that someone would catch us and kill us. I missed my family, and I was hungry. About 15 people went back to our village. They were beaten badly and interrogated. Some ran away again.

People in my village are scared of the army. They kill people slowly. That's why people run away, because they have seen people tortured. My uncle was killed like that. It took him two and a half days to die. I am angry when I think about my people. They don't get to go to school; they have to farm other people's land. Their lives are very difficult. I became a Christian because I believe we deserve a better life.

☥☮✸ॐ✡✝☪

Reflection Questions

• Have you ever experienced harassment, violence, or oppression because of your religion, as Glun Siu did? Have you ever felt the need to hide your religion?

• Are different religions practiced within your extended family? How does this affect your family's relationships? Has this impacted how your family is treated by others?

• Are there people within your own religious tradition that hold extreme views you find troubling? How do you respond to such views?

• Instead of a conflict between religions, Ayat Hussein sees a conflict between extremism in all forms and people who stand up against extremism. What are some ways to address extremism without demonizing people of different religions?

• Are there texts in your religion's holy writings that advocate violence against other groups or glorify war? Are there texts in your religion's holy writings that advocate peace? How do you make sense of these texts and apply them to life today?

• Have you experienced religion as a means of helping you find hope and perseverance in the face of adversity, like the Montagnards in Vietnam? What specific traditions, practices, or holy texts have inspired you most during challenging times?

Resources for Engagement

Where Do I Start?

- Visit a place of worship for a religion different from your own. Contact another religious group in your community to see if you can schedule a visit or if they host an open house—or offer to host an exchange if that group is interested in learning more about your place of worship. See if you can learn about the ways each group contributes to the community and discuss whether there are ways you can support each other's work or partner together.

- Organize an interfaith volunteer project with a local non-profit (such as Habitat for Humanity, a food bank, etc.).

- Research what people in your own religious tradition are doing on an issue you are passionate about, and see how you can build on that work in your local community or place of worship.

- Find out what people in your community are doing on an issue you are passionate about, and get your church/temple/mosque/synagogue involved.

- Share your story of how your faith has shaped your understanding of a particular justice issue. You are invited to share your story on our Facebook page (fb.me/StoriesAcrossReligions), or you may want to organize your own story-sharing event in your community.

Multi-faith Organizations and Resources for Action

- **National Interfaith Alliance:** https://interfaithalliance.org/
  See if there is a local Interfaith Alliance in your community—or if you can help start one!

- **Interfaith Youth Core:** https://www.ifyc.org/
  Connect with this movement to foster interfaith cooperation and understanding on college campuses, and read more stories by people of different faiths on their digital magazine, INTER.

- **Faith Matters Network:** https://www.faithmattersnetwork.org/
  Find resources for prophetic spiritual leaders and connect with other faith leaders organizing social movements.

- **Groundswell Movement:** https://action.groundswell-mvmt.org/
  Start a multi-faith online petition for a cause you care about, or support other interfaith campaigns for justice.

- **Revolutionary Love Project:** https://revolutionarylove.net/
  Promote an ethic of love that challenges the forces of racism, nationalism, and hatred through stories, films, conferences, and other media that equip and inspire activists.

- **Charter for Compassion:** https://charterforcompassion.org/
  Collaborate with others working to create more compassionate communities and sign on to the Charter for Compassion.

- **Our Three Winners Foundation:** https://ourthreewinners.org/
  Address the root causes of racism by raising awareness about implicit bias.

Bridges don't fall from the sky, they don't rise from the ground. People build them.

—Eboo Patel

Proceeds from this book will be donated to Habitat for Humanity of Wake County's Interfaith Build. Every year, more than 20 different faith groups come together to raise funds, organize, and build a home with a local family in Raleigh, North Carolina. This collaboration started in 2011 to commemorate the 10th anniversary of 9/11. One of the original organizers was Farris Barakat, brother of Deah Barakat who was one of the three Muslim students killed in Chapel Hill on February 10, 2015. Diane Faires Beadle, co-editor of this book, was also involved in that first Interfaith Build, and was inspired by the murder of Deah and Yusor and Razan Mohammad Abu-Salha to create a book of interfaith stories. Through your purchase of this book, you support the construction of a safe, decent place to live for a family that could not otherwise afford to purchase their own home. You also support meaningful collaboration between people of different religions, who build relationships and understanding while working together to build this home. For more information on this project, go to https://www.habitatwake.org/faith/interfaith.

Acknowledgments

A special thanks to all the contributors who entrusted their stories to us. We also want to thank the interfaith communities that have inspired us and enriched our understanding, especially Habitat for Humanity of Wake County's Interfaith Build organizing team; the students and teachers of Jaffna College, Sri Lanka; Westminster College, and the University of Richmond. We are both grateful for the many encouraging family members, friends, and colleagues who have shared their wisdom and excitement with us as we brought this project to fruition, especially our Vanderbilt Disciples Women and Michael Beadle. We appreciate friends and colleagues who gave us input on the work in progress, including Cara Gilger, and the countless contacts shared with us as we looked for stories that would offer a diverse range of perspectives.